NYLIFF

THE ESSENTIAL GUIDE TO
HOME COMPUTER SECURITY

BCS, THE CHARTERED INSTITUTE FOR IT

Our mission as BCS, The Chartered Institute for IT, is to enable the information society. We promote wider social and economic progress through the advancement of information technology science and practice. We bring together industry, academics, practitioners and government to share knowledge, promote new thinking, inform the design of new curricula, shape public policy and inform the public.

Our vision is to be a world-class organisation for IT. Our 70,000 strong membership includes practitioners, businesses, academics and students in the UK and internationally. We deliver a range of professional development tools for practitioners and employees. A leading IT qualification body, we offer a range of widely recognised qualifications.

Further Information
BCS The Chartered Institute for IT,
First Floor, Block D,
North Star House, North Star Avenue,
Swindon, SN2 1FA, United Kingdom.
T +44 (0) 1793 417 424
F +44 (0) 1793 417 444
www.bcs.org/contactus

THE ESSENTIAL GUIDE TO HOME COMPUTER SECURITY

Robert R. Rowlingson

Published by British Informatics Society Limited (BISL), a wholly owned subsidiary of BCS The Chartered Institute for IT, First Floor, Block D, North Star House, North Star Avenue, Swindon, SN2 1FA, UK.
www.bcs.org

ISBN: 978-1-906124-69-4
PDF ISBN: 978-1-78017-108-1
ePUB ISBN: 978-1-78017-109-8
Kindle ISBN: 978-1-78017-110-4

British Cataloguing in Publication Data.
A CIP catalogue record for this book is available at the British Library.

Disclaimer:
The views expressed in this book are of the author(s) and do not necessarily reflect the views of BCS or BISL except where explicitly stated as such. Although every care has been taken by the authors and BISL in the preparation of the publication, no warranty is given by the authors or BISL as publisher as to the accuracy or completeness of the information contained within it and neither the authors nor BISL shall be responsible or liable for any loss or damage whatsoever arising by virtue of such information or any instructions or advice contained within this publication or by any of the aforementioned.

Typeset by Lapiz Digital Services, Chennai, India.
Printed and bound by CPI Group (UK) Ltd., Croydon, CR0 4YY

CONTENTS

ABBREVIATIONS

CA	Certificate Authority
CERT	Computer Emergency Response Team
CPU	Central Processing Unit
EFS	Encrypted File System
HDD	Hard Disk Drive
HTML	HyperText Mark-up Language
HTTP	HyperText Transfer Protocol
IP	Internet Protocol
ISP	Internet Service Provider
MBSA	Microsoft® Baseline Security Analyser
MIME	Multi-purpose Internet Mail Extension
OS	Operating System
PC	Personal Computer
PGP	Pretty Good Privacy
PIN	Personal Identification Number
RAT	Remote Access Trojan
RSACi	Recreational Software Advisory Council on the Internet
SSID	Service Set Identifier
SSL	Secure Sockets Layer
UAC	User Account Control
URL	Uniform Resource Locator
USB	Universal Serial Bus
VBA	Visual Basic for Applications®
VBS	Visual Basic® Script
WEP	Wired Equivalent Privacy
WPA	Wi-Fi Protected Access

USEFUL WEBSITES

www.anti-bullyingalliance.org.uk	Anti-bullying Alliance
www.antivirusworld.com	AntiVirusWorld
www.auditmypc.com	Auditmypc. Firewall test.
www.avg.com	AVG Technologies. Free anti-virus software.
www.av-test.org	AV-Test GmbH
www.banksafeonline.org.uk	Bank Safe Online
www.bcs.org	BCS, The Chartered Institute for IT
www.cert.org	Computer Emergency Response Team (Carnegie Mellon University Software Engineering Institute)
www.chatdanger.com	Child International ChatDanger
www.childline.org.uk	NSPCC ChildLine
www.childnet-int.org	Childnet International. For parents and children.
www.cybermentors.org.uk	Help to prevent cyberbullying.
www.direct.gov.uk/en/YoungPeople/CrimeAndJustice/KeepingSafe/DG_10027670	Staying safe online.
www.download.com	CNET Download.com. For security software.
explore.live.com/windows-live-family-safety	Windows Live Family Safety Software
www.getsafeonline.org	Get Safe Online
getvirushelp.com	GetVirusHelp.com
www.google.com/security	Google Inc. Security information.

www.grc.com	Gibson Research Corporation. Security advice.
www.hushmail.com	Hush Communications Canada Inc.
www.ico.gov.uk	Information Commissioner's Office
www.itsecurityportal.com	IT Security Portal. IT security news and information.
www.iwf.org.uk	The Internet Watch Foundation
www.keypass.info	Keypass
www.kidsmart.org.uk	Kidsmart
www.lavasoft.com	Lavasoft. Free anti-virus software.
www.legislation.hmso.gov.uk	Lawful Business Practice Regulations
www.microsoft.com/en-gb/security	Microsoft Safety and Security Centre
www.nspcc.org.uk	National Society for the Prevention of Cruelty to Children
www.privacy.net	Privacy.net
www.safekids.com	SafeKids.com
www.saferinternet.org	Insafe. Internet safety.
www.safer-networking.org	Safer Networking Ltd
safety.yahoo.com	Yahoo! Safety. Internet safety for families.
www.sans.org	The SANS Institute
www.securityfocus.com	Security Focus
www.spamcop.net	Cisco Systems SpamCop
www.thepcmanwebsite.com	The PC Man Website. Security advice.
www.thinkuknow.co.uk	Child Exploitation and Online Protection Centre
www.v3.co.uk	Incisive Media. IT and security news.
www.virusbtn.com	Virus Bulletin Ltd
www.vmyths.com	Virus Myths
www.yahooligans.com	Yahoo! Kids

PREFACE

I first had the idea for this book not long after I started working in information security. I was asked to write a guide to the ideas and technologies of information security for an IT literate audience who, like me, were new to security. So I had to think carefully about how I wanted to communicate it and how, if it were me reading the guide, I could get the most out of it. As I wrote this it became increasingly clear that all IT users had to understand security, not only because our workplaces needed to be secure, but so did our homes. There was little information for those who might not call themselves IT literate, so there was also a clear need to provide a guide to information security for home users. This was some years ago. Since then it seems that everything has changed but nothing has changed. Technology has changed radically, software has evolved at pace, and our use and dependence on the internet has become even more intense. But the need to protect ourselves from security threats and vulnerabilities has not changed. The need for this book remains.

Nowadays there is a lot more information for home users but information security is too often thought of as a technical subject. The solution to security problems is seen as software products and technologies. This puts off many novices and home users. In fact, security is more about people and processes and requires an underlying appreciation of risk. Without understanding of these factors, even security products may not provide the security needed.

My aim for this book is to help those who want to understand what security is really about, and enable them to use that understanding to take sensible measures to reduce their risk. A simple way to do this might have been to provide a set of things to do, tools to run, options to select and so on, but this would have just put a sticking plaster on the problem. What I really want you to take away from this book is a philosophy of security, how to think about it, by understanding the risks, the threats and the vulnerabilities, so that as IT changes and information security evolves, you are equipped to make the right decisions and can confidently protect yourself, your information and your family.

I would like to thank Nic Peeling for giving me the opportunity to research information security and figure it out in my own way. I would like to thank Cath, who has seen me through the ups and downs of writing as well as growing our family in the meantime! I would also like to thank the BCS for supporting this project and their championing of security in so many ways.

In theory, any computer could be used at home, but this book focuses on the most common: Microsoft® Windows®-based systems. Much of the general advice in this book is relevant whatever the computer used.

I have gone against convention in this book by not providing glossy screenshots. Although these can sometimes look effective, I am not convinced how easy they are to use in practice. Furthermore, they can often differ from version to version. It is better just to follow the option labels – which may be buttons, tabs, drop-down menus or whatever. When you get a security problem or a new piece of software you wish to secure, there may be no screenshots anywhere to sort it out for you. You will have to look at the menus, the options and so forth to make a sensible choice. The convention in this book is to show a sequence of options you need to select, in order, such as:

Start→Menu Item→Choice means click the Windows Start button (bottom left of screen), then click the 'Menu Item' and then find and click 'Choice'. Simply look for each element of the sequence as you go through the operation. Look in menus, tabs, command boxes or wherever, and you should find the next step in the sequence.

It is not the purpose of this book to review and recommend security products. These change rapidly and the best for you today may not be the best tomorrow, and may not be right for other readers. Many quality commercial products, and good free tools, are available, but security is not just about technology. Even with good security software you need an understanding of the principles of security. That is what this book is about.

And finally, let's be careful out there!

Robert R. Rowlingson
My blog on Home Computer Security can be viewed at
www.homeinfosec.blogspot.com

INTRODUCTION

Computers and the internet are wonderful modern phenomena that we just can't do without. We are becoming dependent on them in every aspect of our lives: for work, for play, for shopping, for banking, for communicating, for learning. Whatever we do with them, and however they can benefit our daily lives, there is one unfortunate consequence that we cannot escape. They are not secure.

Communications over the internet are not secure. Emails are not confidential. They pass through many computers before reaching their destination. Internet shopping is not secure. Our credit card numbers are transmitted around the world and stored on company computers directly connected to the internet where they can become an attractive target to criminal hackers. Likewise, internet banking is not secure. If someone guesses or obtains an account's password, the account details become visible and rogue transactions become possible.

I am not going to start this book with a call to paranoia. Nothing is 100 per cent secure. Our phones can be tapped, our houses can be burgled, our credit cards forged and so on *ad infinitum*. But we are happy to talk about our most private matters on the phone, our houses generally do not resemble Fort Knox and we shop until we drop with our credit cards. The reason is we have a 'feel' for the risks involved. We have some experience and confidence as to whether the security will fail. We are reasonably relaxed about the impact it will have on us if it does.

Few of us understand the modern interconnected digital world very well. Few of us want to understand it well, or have the time to understand it. Nevertheless, we know there are risks to everything in life and that the internet reaches deep into our homes, bringing threats to our children, to our bank balances and to our privacy. We have no choice but to face these risks. The threats from the internet are very personal. We cannot afford to be complacent. However technologically naive we are, or want to be, we cannot ignore these threats any more than we can ignore the threats of being burgled or defrauded. We take simple and effective measures against the latter threats: we lock our doors, we check our credit card statements and bank balances. We also need to take the right measures for our home computer security.

This book is for everyone who wants to understand the new threats that come with the internet territory, and wants to address them in as simple and effective way as possible.

Most books on computer security tackle the subject in one of two ways. Either they provide the technical background to help people with a good understanding of computers develop an even better understanding of computer security, or they help companies implement security in their organisation. Basically, companies employ staff who have the computer security expertise in the first type of book to ensure their company information is kept secure using the ideas in the second type of book. Corporate information security is big business and there is a shortage of qualified staff. This may explain why very little has been written to help the average home PC user. There are many reasonably priced PC security software packages that can, and should, be used by home users. There is also a lot of good, free, security software that could be used instead. There are many good ideas and practices being applied in large companies that could, and should, be used by home users. This book is for people with little computer knowledge who want some simple and effective measures to secure their home PC. This book is about the sensible, practical countermeasures that we can take to make our home PCs secure and keep them that way.

To understand risks requires an understanding of some basic PC and internet technology. To put security in place to counter the threats requires a small investment of time. Even taking the practical measures suggested in this book will not produce a Fort Knox PC. Nothing is 100 per cent secure. But you can avoid some of the biggest threats; you can be more resistant to hostile attack; you will be aware when your privacy is threatened. We all should have the digital equivalent of walls, gates, locks and bars. We should all have the digital 'common sense' equivalent to not leaving our credit cards lying around; our PIN next to our cash card; or our car keys in the pub. We can raise our level of security so that we are far less likely to be the ones who suffer from the consequences of internet insecurity. For without being paranoid, we are all at risk, and increasing numbers of home computer users are suffering. Make sure that doesn't include you!

1 INFORMATION SECURITY

When we talk about home computer security what we are really concerned about is the information stored on our home computers, the information we access on the World Wide Web, or receive by way of emails or other messages. Computer security is usually called information security, to show that it is the information we are trying to secure, and not the physical computer itself.

WHAT IS INFORMATION SECURITY?

Information security is like any other form of security, but with a twist. We wish to protect something that we value: information. The difference is that information exists on our computers, in electronic form, as documents, photos, programs, pictures, emails and other files. This information is transported between computers, and is easily and quickly duplicated or broadcast. Electronic information is not like many of the things that we know how to secure. It is intangible. It can be copied, distributed and destroyed with the click of a mouse button in the blink of an eye. This makes it difficult to protect. We cannot see it to protect it, we cannot see what is happening to it nor what we need to defend it against.

While information exists in electronic form, in transit or on a hard drive or memory stick, we need to protect it from things like theft, destruction, fraud, unauthorised use or unauthorised disclosure. This is exactly like our need to protect our property in the physical domain. In order to protect something we need to understand what we are protecting it against, how we can protect it and how strongly we need to protect it. How much we protect something usually depends on two things: how much we value it and how much risk we are prepared to take. Risk can never be completely eliminated, there is always some residual risk.

It is difficult to place a value on information. It may have little monetary value but immense personal value. What value do you put on your collection of photographs of your children growing up? If they are stored, digitally, on your computer you might think it worth spending time to ensure they were not damaged, deleted or accessed by someone you do not trust.

Information has to be protected against attack from outsiders, attack from insiders, and innocent mistakes from users. In information security these are known as threats, or threat agents. Information is protected against threats using countermeasures. Our level of risk exposure is an important judgement call. Our understanding of the threats and vulnerabilities helps us make this decision.

In information security we have to be aware of the current threats to, and vulnerabilities of, our information. And act accordingly.

Anything about information that you wish to protect, any property of information, is the subject of information security. So what properties of information do we need to consider countermeasures for?

Confidentiality

Information we wish to keep personal, private or secret is confidential. Examples of information we should keep confidential are passwords and credit card numbers. Confidentiality is a major problem in information security because it is so easy to make electronic copies, and all too easy to move them around.

Integrity

We usually think of integrity as honesty or trustworthiness. Information security uses it in roughly the same way. Something has integrity if you are certain that it has not been changed in any way from its original form. Integrity means you can trust that the information that you receive is what was sent to you: that you can trust that the file you are reading does contain the text that appears on the screen.

Authenticity

Something is authentic when it is exactly what it claims to be. A forged painting is something that lacks authenticity. A copy of the Mona Lisa is not by Da Vinci. The two dollar bill is not legal tender. Neither is authentic. A computer user may prove their authenticity (i.e. who they say they are) by means of a PIN or password. An example of where authenticity is important is if you are buying something from a website. You need to be confident that the site is a bona fide (authentic) business that will fulfil its side of the transaction. The website needs to know that you are the owner of an authentic credit card in order to buy goods.

Availability

No computer is 100 per cent reliable. At some point all computers will have 'down time' when they are no longer available to provide the information they were programmed to. One of the main reasons to keep your computer secure is to ensure that it remains available to you. Lack of availability is also extremely important in the world of e-commerce. Websites are often hit with what are called 'Denial of Service' attacks. These are security attacks with the goal of taking down their target machines by flooding them with traffic from the internet.

Timeliness

If information reaches you late it can have fateful consequences. To track stock market prices, for example, up to the minute information is critical. If someone could delay important business news so that they had a time advantage to trade shares before others, it could be highly profitable to that person!

Suitability

Information has to be suitable for its audience. A TV programme, a newspaper, a magazine article or a lecture is usually designed to be of interest to a certain group of people. This might be a very large group (e.g. for a big sporting event) or a very small group (e.g. for a presentation on an obscure topic). In the non-computer world we use our experience of the media, and perhaps read reviews, to determine whether or not what we wish to view, read or hear is suitable. On the internet this is much more difficult. The information available changes rapidly, reviews are hard to come by and, unfortunately, there is information available that may not only be unsuitable for us, but, more importantly, for children. As adults we can change channels or move to a different website if we find something unpalatable, but children could be traumatised by viewing unsuitable information. So whatever our views on censorship or the appropriateness of different types of information we will need to ensure that the information on our home computers is suitable for the whole family to use.

PRINCIPLES OF GOOD SECURITY

The principles of good security can help to guide us in making good security decisions. There are a few basic ones worth understanding. They form the basis of many of the specific protection measures you will see later in this book.

Security is only as strong as the weakest link
One weak point is sufficient for security to be broken. The implication of this is that we have to be able to recognise and address the main weaknesses we find in our security.

Be aware of the threats and vulnerabilities
Following on from this is the need to maintain awareness of the threats, vulnerabilities and potential countermeasures relevant to your computing use. This knowledge is needed to find and address the weakest link, and also to keep up to date with the rapidly changing environment for security.

Apply defence-in-depth
The need to ensure a sound defence contributes to the next principle. Just like a castle has a moat, thick walls and knights firing arrows, a computer also needs defence-in-depth. The principle of defence-in-depth is designed to ensure that security cannot be circumvented by the failure of one countermeasure alone.

Ensure users have the 'least privilege'
Every user has some ability to change, or configure, their user experience. However, the more power they have to change things, the more risk there is of a mistake being made, or of a piece of software using that power as a form of attack. The professional's approach is to give users the 'least privilege' they need to use the PC as they wish, but no more.

Use defence-in-breadth
As well as defence-in-depth we also have the principle of defence-in-breadth. This is the need to use a range of countermeasures of different types. We need a balanced set of procedural measures, personnel measures, physical security measures as well as technical measures. Technical measures alone, even in-depth technical measures, can often be circumvented using non-technical means.

Trust

A lot of security is 'all in the mind', because security is typically about trust. If we trust too much we put ourselves at risk. This is obviously true of any walk of human life. When it comes to our online life, caution and suspicion are the operative words. Trust should be endowed sparingly and only when any mistaken trust cannot hurt us. Do not trust anything that seems too good to be true and always try to obtain corroboration for any information you rely on.

Security is a process not a product

There is a tendency to believe that, in this modern technological age, there is a technological 'fix' for weak security, that finding the right product will deliver the required security. But technology can only be part of security. Achieving security is a process of understanding threats, implementing countermeasures to those threats, monitoring and reviewing the security posture, and maintaining an evolving set of countermeasures. Those countermeasures will certainly include technology, but they should also include sensible procedures and practices to reduce risk and to mitigate the impact of a security compromise.

Security is a trade-off

Putting in place security measures brings a cost. It might cost money, it will certainly cost time. In principle the more time and the more money you can spend and the more intelligence you can put into your security, the more secure you will be. But this is a trade-off, your time and money might be better spent doing something else. What level of security do you really want or need? Is it worth the effort to achieve that level of security? Sometimes security is also a trade-off on usability. An anti-virus program can slow your PC down. A filter program or firewall may block access to the internet unnecessarily. So security is a trade-off and you need to understand how much effort to put into it, what trade-offs are involved and how secure you really want to be.

Risks need to be managed, they cannot be eliminated

Our last, but by no means least, principle of good security is that it should be based on an understanding of risk. The level of risk being taken dictates the level of security required. The remainder of this chapter looks at the components of risk and how we can perform a risk assessment to guide us in our choice of countermeasures.

There are two important factors that need to be considered whenever risk is mentioned: threats and vulnerabilities. A threat is someone or something with the potential to do harm. A vulnerability is a weakness in security that may allow a compromise to happen. We apply countermeasures to prevent a threat from exploiting a vulnerability to cause a compromise.

COUNTERMEASURES

Fortunately, there are numerous countermeasures you can use to implement home computer security. Generally they fall into four categories.

Physical countermeasures

Physical countermeasures include all the ways of securing the physical components or locations of information. They might include locking the doors of rooms containing computers to prevent unauthorised use, and bolting laptops to tables to prevent theft.

Technical countermeasures
Technical countermeasures use computer software to provide defence. Important examples include anti-virus software, which detects whether a virus is on your PC, and personal firewalls, which help to prevent attacks via your internet connection. Other technical measures include secure access control, the use of good passwords and ensuring that users do not have unnecessary Administrator rights on their PC.

Process countermeasures
Good processes can ensure that security operates effectively. An important example is the backing up of data. This is when copies of data are made, and stored carefully, so that if the original is lost or deleted, a back-up version is available. Making a back-up is an essential activity in computer security.

Personnel countermeasures
Personnel countermeasures involve people and their knowledge, attitude and understanding of computer security issues. In business, the main approach is to train staff to understand the security risks that exist and their responsibilities towards their employer's systems. For home computer users the situation is very similar. All users need to be aware of the main security threats and what they should do to avoid the wide variety of potential problems. A good starting point is to understand the principles of good security.

Specific essential and recommended countermeasures
There are a number of important and essential countermeasures that every home user should deploy and these are discussed in some detail in the chapters indicated. They are:

- installing and running anti-virus software (see Chapter 6);
- setting up user accounts so that users do not have Administrator access (see Chapter 2);
- installing and running a firewall (see Chapter 4);
- choosing and using good passwords (see Chapter 3);
- backing up the files you do not want to lose (see Chapter 3);
- keeping software up to date, especially the operating system and internet browser, so that they have the latest security fixes (see Chapter 3);
- being aware of possible threats and being alert to new threats (see Chapter 3).

It is important to understand the risks you are taking and be particularly careful when downloading applications, opening attachments and using the web for financial transactions.

Information security is a rapidly changing area. New attacks emerge and some are so novel that they weren't even imagined before they appeared. New defensive technologies appear. Recommendations and priorities will change from month to month. As well as knowing and undertaking these essential countermeasures we need to understand the principles and philosophy of good security in order to be forewarned and forearmed to the new threat landscape of tomorrow. We cannot just rely on technology.

THREATS TO INFORMATION SECURITY

We have learned that the purpose of information security is to apply countermeasures to effectively reduce the likelihood and impact of a compromise. Computer security attacks often make high-profile news stories.

The following are some types of compromises you need to have in the back of your mind whenever you use your PC or the internet, or are thinking about security measures. You have probably heard of some of them.

- **Viruses** – These are basically pieces of software designed to be able to make copies of themselves, autonomously (known as worms) or with a little human assistance. They can only infect your computer if you run an infected program, open an infected document or read an infected email. They come in many shapes and sizes. As of 2011, over 100,000 different variants have been reported by companies whose products detect them. Viruses perform a range of actions once established on a new host: they might detect keyboard presses to find passwords or banking numbers; they might divert a user's browser to a specific and unwanted website; or they might disrupt the use of the computer or delete files. Basically they can do anything, and so are a grave danger and one of the biggest nightmares for the home computer user. Unfortunately many people first become aware of viruses when their computer becomes infected. More information about viruses and what you can do about them is given in Chapter 6.

- **Identity theft** – This is the crime of appropriating someone's credentials and personal information in order to obtain money or goods fraudulently. It is not a new crime, a forged signature on a stolen cheque is a form of identity theft. However, the threat is now much bigger and more widespread than ever, and it is increasing. The rise in use of the internet has allowed people to obtain useful identity information from a distance and then to use it in transactions at a distance. No face-to-face contact is required. The cybercriminal's remoteness reduces the chances of detection and of getting your money returned, or your reputation restored.

  The targets for credential theft include the obvious, like credit card numbers, bank account details and social security numbers, as well as the not quite so obvious, like address, former addresses, employer details, mother's maiden name etc. All of these can help to build a forged identity or to guess weak passwords. Sensitive information should not be given out unless absolutely necessary, and then only to a secure website that you trust.

- **Phishing** – One of the fastest growing scams in recent years is known as 'phishing'. This involves the receipt of an email, usually purporting to come from a bank, which asks you to confirm your personal details, such as your online account name and password. The emails helpfully contain a link to your bank's website. Unfortunately this is actually a link to a fake website made to resemble the bank's website. The owner of the fake website can then obtain your bank account details and its contents.

- **Cyberstalking and cyberbullying** – These are crimes where the intent is harassment and intimidation. Again it has parallels to the non-computer domain. They comprise such things as abusive emails, threatening messages and all manner of pestering communications methods. Our increasingly online lifestyle makes these crimes personal and intrusive, and they can be extremely distressing especially for the young or vulnerable. There is also the risk that cyber activity turns into real-world harassment and that the perpetrator may proceed to an even more serious crime.

- **Financial scams** – Various scams have been developed over many years to deceive us into parting with our money. One such fraud, the so-called '419' scam, usually involves a bogus claim that the perpetrator is attempting to export a large sum of money from a corrupt country and needs your help in the way of your bank account details. The money (millions of dollars supposedly) will be paid into your account and you will receive a healthy fee in return. The only outcome of this scam is the emptying of any bank account that falls into the hands of the perpetrator. A similar approach is taken by operators of the lottery scam. They send you an email or text message stating that you have won a large lottery prize. All you have to do to collect it is to pay a small fee. The prize, of course, does not exist and the lottery company is just a front for criminals.

- **Botnets** – These are used for another type of attack known as a 'Distributed Denial of Service' attack. This uses home PCs as the source of an attack rather than as the main victim. The attacker infiltrates many computers and installs software that performs the traffic flooding. These computers are known as zombies. Many innocent users' home PCs are taken over to become zombies and are formed into a 'botnet'. These attacks have been launched against many high-profile web businesses. Basically their websites are flooded with so much internet traffic that legitimate users are unable to access the sites and the businesses lose sales as a result. The attacks are successful, principally because they are distributed, that is they are launched from many different computers across the internet at the same time. The overload of traffic does not originate from the attacker's machine.

The threat from cybercriminals

To be a threat to information security requires someone to have some degree of skill, knowledge, access and resources. This gives them the capability to cause a compromise. Hackers, for example, have a high degree of skill and knowledge in the use of computers and the ways in which security measures can be subverted. Insiders have specific knowledge and access to systems that gives them an opportunity to cause a compromise or to make innocent mistakes.

Cybercrimes are generally thought to be growing in number. Many are problems to businesses and large organisations but some can affect us as home PC users. The main objective of cybercriminals is to obtain your money or your identity. With your identity they could commit a crime in your name, apply for a passport or rent a property. With your identity they can obtain your money, or they may use it to obtain money from someone else, such as a bank, by pretending to be you. In the former case you are hit financially and in the latter your credit rating and financial stability is put at risk. Cybercriminals use a number of techniques to meet their objectives.

Criminal hackers

Possibly the most well-known threat to information security is the hacker. The term 'hacker' actually has many meanings. It not only refers to people who try to break into computers maliciously but is also used for computer programmers who can write effective and efficient code. The types of hacker we are concerned about in this book are often referred to as 'criminal hackers'. They aim to break the law by penetrating systems, stealing information, defacing web pages, attacking businesses etc. They are a particular type of cybercriminal. Sometimes they may hack for financial gain. Sometimes they hack for no obvious personal benefit except the ability to demonstrate their technical prowess to their peer group.

To defend against hackers we have to understand what they do. Their first goal is access. Once a hacker has accessed your computer and can run programs on it then he or she has control. In principle a hacker can have as much control of your computer as if he or she was sitting right in front of it. Your files can be read, copied or deleted. Your email can be read and your email account used. Your keyboard can be bugged so that every keystroke is recorded to find passwords and credit card numbers. Even your camera and microphone can be subverted and used as recording devices to spy on you. Of course the hacker isn't sitting by his computer doing this personally, he or she installs software to do the job. This software is known as a Trojan horse. So if we can defend against external penetration of our system we can also do a good job of protecting against malicious software.

How do hackers hack?

How do hackers penetrate systems? There are several ways. The first way is quite straightforward. They just send you some malicious software and you run it without realising what it does. When you think about it, how do we know any software does exactly what we expect it to? The simple answer is that we don't. If we buy software in a box from a shop we can probably be pretty sure that someone has checked it out, and that the copy we bought is the same as every other, and that if there was something seriously wrong it would have been reported, but if we download software from a website we do not have that assurance. Any piece of software is potentially malicious. You cannot just blindly trust every source of software. The internet has become a veritable lucky dip of free software. Much of it is good, respectable application software, but check its provenance. Are you downloading it from the website of its creators? Does the site seem valid, long-lived? Is the company providing updates and bug fixes? If not, what confidence can you place in it?

There is a variety of ways that such malicious software can infect you. It could install itself without your knowledge: perhaps it was hidden on a USB stick or came as an unwanted by-product of a web page (known as a drive-by download). It could have been an email attachment that you thought was benign, or gave the impression of being benign. The message here is beware of clicking on unknown files or running new software unless you are given some indicator, or have some confidence, of it likely to being safe.

The second way a hacker might attack is through what are known as probes. Basically he or she sends network signals that issue requests for information about your computer. This might give some clues as to how open it is to particular types of attack. In other words, what the vulnerabilities are on your PC. Computers attached to networks or running websites are set up to communicate with the internet in a number of different ways and an attacker will choose one if the probe finds a weakness or opportunity.

Why do hackers hack?

Hackers hack for a variety of reasons. Perhaps the foremost explanation is that they get excitement in demonstrating their ability to overcome internet security. They also get a buzz from sharing the news of their exploits with their peers. This peer judgement is often a stimulant to further attacks. These are the most technically proficient hackers but not necessarily the most dangerous. In many cases they are not intentionally aiming to cause damage or disrupt business. However, this lack of intent is no excuse. Even the simplest act of computer intrusion can cost a company a lot of time and money to investigate, and distress to a home user.

Others hack for direct commercial gain. They attempt to steal data like passwords, credit card numbers and social security numbers. They then use this information in further criminal acts such as ordering goods, accessing accounts and generating fake IDs. These are the principal enemies of the home computer user.

Why would a hacker hack me?

In addition to the criminal reasons described above, another reason why your PC may be useful to an attacker is if he or she is trying to hide evidence of their criminal activity. If someone wants to break into an important or well-protected website, then doing so directly from their own computer might allow the defenders of that site to locate the source of the attack and thereby alert the police. If the attacker has taken over somebody else's computer it becomes much more difficult to trace the original perpetrator of the activity. The criminal will probably set up a complex chain of controlled computers, and will probably locate these in different countries to make it doubly difficult for the authorities, not only to trace him or her, but to gather the evidence for prosecution. The upshot of all this is that your computer could be the unwitting accomplice in a major crime.

An attacker may not be targeting the data on your computer. They may purely be interested in the fact that it has internet access that they can make use of in further attacks. They may try to use your PC and many others as dummy machines in a concerted attack. Alternatively, they may want control of your computer as a way into a more lucrative target such as your work network. This is reported as being the underlying cause of a publicised intrusion into Microsoft®. The attackers penetrated the home PC of a Microsoft® employee who used his PC to work from home, and the attackers used it to access the internal Microsoft® company network. Thus the attackers played leap-frog in order to reach a more attractive target.

Trusted insiders

Compromises can also be caused by trusted 'insiders' who abuse the trust placed in them. The military refer to such people as traitors. An insider is someone who has legitimate access to a computer. They are on the inside so they are often trusted in some way. This can give them capabilities beyond those of the external hacker, making traitors one of the most difficult threats to counter. In companies, the computer system manager, for example, is one of the most trusted individuals when it comes to the IT systems. If there are problems with the system manager and, say, he or she has to be sacked, they have the power to do untold damage in revenge.

There are similar issues for home PC users. You may have people, acquaintances, staff perhaps, who you allow into your home, but you wouldn't necessarily trust them with your bank account PIN or the keys to your safety deposit box. Likewise they should not be trusted too much when it comes to your computer and its information.

Accidents

However, it is not just criminal hackers who cause compromises – they are just the most visible and seem to get the most publicity. Compromises are often caused by accidents by legitimate users. In some sense you are the biggest threat to the information on your computer. One wrong move and you could delete the lot!

Defence against accidents can be tricky. Most people at some time in their computing lives have deleted files they didn't mean to. Sometimes they can be retrieved. In Microsoft® Windows® computers, a deleted file is not actually removed from the disk. It is just transferred from its original folder to the waste bin or deleted folder, and can easily be restored if the waste bin has not been emptied. Even if it is 'permanently' deleted (by deleting it from the deleted folder) the bits on the hard disk that constitute that particular file will remain in place until they are overwritten by additional data, so even in this case they may be retrievable. If you send an email accidentally, however, there is very little you can do to get that email back. It is quite odd that we are asked for confirmation when we delete something but not when we send an email.

VULNERABILITIES

The threats we have discussed above exploit vulnerabilities (weaknesses). Without vulnerabilities, successful attacks would not be possible. One of the key things in our understanding of risk is to understand our vulnerabilities and how to minimise them.

Out-of-date software

Whilst software doesn't have a sell-by date as such, it does become weaker, and more vulnerable, as time goes by. Modern software contains millions of lines of code and there are always bugs in such code. Some of these bugs will have security consequences and can be exploited by hackers to gain access to systems, or by virus writers to create infectious viruses. Thus one of the first security tasks is to ensure that your software is updated. Most software vendors will issue updates and security 'patches' that fix new security weaknesses found in their software. How to ensure your software is updated is addressed in Chapter 3.

Users with the power of Administrators

Administrator is the term used for the person who has the most control, or privileges, on a computer. They have the power to change settings, alter security levels, manage other users' files and privileges, load and run new software etc. With this power comes vulnerability. If another person, or a piece of software, gains this power they can instigate a successful attack. Thus it is important that a PC is set up so that each user has an account that does not have Administrator privileges, and that users use these accounts to browse the web, check email and to perform all their other day-to-day activities. An Administrator account should be reserved for occasional use whenever changes to the PC require the extra authority. This is further addressed in Chapter 2.

Software flaws
Compromises can be caused by flaws in a system. In other words the system does not behave in the way we expect it to. For example, if we are using encryption to keep our emails confidential, but unknown to us our software is not actually performing the encryption, then we are still at risk of compromise even though we thought we had taken appropriate countermeasures. Flaws often emerge because of the complexity of modern software. The different programs we use can also interact in unexpected ways and expose vulnerabilities in our security.

Vulnerabilities of the mind
Vulnerabilities can exist in all parts of a computer system and beyond into the network and the communications channels. They are certainly present in software, but they are also present in users. There are many problems that have little to do with the computer, but with us, the people who use them. We have vulnerabilities that can be exploited by an attacker, for example greed, gullibility, naivety. Crooked scams that have been around for years exploit people's weaknesses. Internet scams are no different. We can be duped by convincing people (this is known as social engineering), but the vulnerability they exploit is in our minds.

Breaking golden rules
Compromises can occur if we break our own rules. One of the biggest rules of email security is 'thou shalt not double-click on email attachments'. Double-clicking on email attachments is extremely risky. Attachments are a very common way of spreading viruses. An email may appear benign, it might even come from a friend or colleague, but the attachment can contain a virus, and running it, by double-clicking, will set it off, not only to replicate and transmit itself to further victims, but also perhaps to delete or corrupt data and programs on your computer. If we decide that we should not run email attachments, but then take a risk by doing so, we are at fault if a malicious piece of software lurks behind it. Another golden rule is 'never tell anyone your password'. This is another rule that is often broken. Better awareness of the risks of breaking these rules is the only way to tackle this. We will learn a lot more about these in later chapters.

Weak passwords
Passwords exemplify the notion that a security countermeasure can also be a vulnerability. A password prevents people who don't know the password from accessing information, but this is only true if the password is strong (i.e. one that cannot be guessed or otherwise easily cracked). Weak passwords are like no security at all and are a major vulnerability. Help in choosing good passwords is given in Chapter 3.

Rogue software

The presence of rogue software is a serious vulnerability. Compromises can also be caused by rogue software known as Trojan horses. Such software masquerades as useful software but performs nefarious actions. One type of Trojan horse can allow your PC to be controlled, remotely, by an attacker from anywhere on the internet. Others cause havoc with files or email themselves out to multiple recipients. Trojan horses are often installed on a victim's computer as a consequence of a virus infection. A nasty form of Trojan is the so-called 'keyboard sniffer'. This monitors what is typed into the keyboard and tries to relay information, such as credit card numbers and passwords, back to its controller. Further details are provided in Chapter 6.

Communications

The vast majority of internet communications is performed 'in the clear'. That is to say that there is no attempt to conceal them or their contents as they cross the internet. Any internet communication can pass through numerous machines en route. All communications will certainly go through your Internet Service Provider (ISP) for example. Thus there is a vulnerability to interception. If you use a wireless connection (Wi-Fi), then there is a risk that your communications could be intercepted. Currently it is not perceived as a major risk that criminals will 'wire-tap' your internet connection, but there are ways and means that it can be done. Some communications, including your Wi-Fi and transactions with secure sites, can be encrypted. This is covered in future chapters.

RISK ASSESSMENT

Now we know what can go wrong with information security, we understand some possible compromises and we know we can use a range of countermeasures to prevent compromises. The next things we need to know are whether we need to bother with countermeasures, and if so which ones. The issue here is risk. We need a risk assessment to answer these questions. Good security is all about managing risk.

Understanding risk

Before we can perform a risk assessment we need to know (or at least estimate) two things. What is the likelihood of a compromise and what is the degree of damage or pain that such a compromise would cause us if it occurred? If the likelihood of a compromise is low, then we may feel that is not worth investing time and money to prevent it. Similarly, if the amount of damage a compromise could cause us is small, then we may not need to do anything about it. This is exactly the same trade-off we pose ourselves with 'normal' physical security. If we live in a high crime neighbourhood or have a lot of expensive items to protect we may well invest in a burglar alarm. On the other hand, when I was a student with only a few possessions, I did not take out insurance against them being stolen.* Risk is a matter of chance. The $64,000 question is: how likely is a compromise? We would like to know the answer to this because it allows us to decide how much effort we should put into the countermeasures. How much effort you personally put into your information security will depend on your perception of risk and of impact. The impact of

---

*Nevertheless, on one occasion I was burgled so my risk assessment was probably wrong!

insecurity is the value that the information has to you, or the cost of replacing it (perhaps in time, perhaps in money).

If you are a light internet user, then the likelihood of some sort of security compromise is probably lower than for an intensive user. If you are not using your credit cards to make internet purchases, have no children browsing the web and can tolerate some downtime on your internet access, then the impact of any compromise is likely to be low. Consequently you may be more relaxed about your security posture and may put less effort into your countermeasures rather than the full gamut of defensive techniques.

If, on the other hand, your children use the web, you do a lot of internet shopping, exchange private or confidential emails and rely on your PC for business, then the risk of a compromise may be higher and the impact of a compromise could be considerable. If this profile resembles you, it would be advisable to 'circle the wagons' and take as many measures recommended in this book that you can find the time for.

We can now perform a risk assessment. Using the above description we can come up with simple definitions of three types of user – low risk, medium risk and high risk – depending on their home computer use. Whichever category you are in gives an indication of the degree of risk you are taking and thus how much effort you should consider putting into the appropriate countermeasures. Remember these are just approximations.

Low-risk user
There will not be many people in this category:

- No children use the computer.
- No use of e-commerce, such as shopping on the web; no e-banking.
- No critical use of the home PC (e.g. for business).

Medium-risk user
One or more of the following is true:

- Children occasionally have supervised access to the computer.
- Regular use of e-commerce (but not e-banking).
- Use of non-browser applications, such as instant messaging, file sharing programs etc.

High-risk user
One or more of the following is true:

- Home PC used for business.
- PC used for e-banking, online auctions, payments or share trading.
- Any network or remote access to the PC.
- Others have unsupervised access to the PC (e.g. children, friends, colleagues).

Low-risk users, at a bare minimum, should still implement the main measures described below and stay aware of new risks as they arise. Medium-risk users should, in addition, try to focus countermeasures on risks related to their specific use of the PC, especially with regard to any children. High-risk users have to implement the most countermeasures and ensure that security is uppermost in their minds as they use and manage their home PCs. As a very rough 'rule of thumb', an investment in information security of around 10 per cent of the time spent using the computer is probably a good idea, or at least a good target, but less is OK if you are a low-risk user as long as you are confidently deploying the essential measures listed in the above section 'Specific essential and recommended countermeasures'.

SUMMARY

We know what information security is about and we know how and why we are insecure. We have an understanding of the degree of risk we are taking and therefore a rough idea of how serious we should be in ensuring security. This book is about the sensible, practical countermeasures that we can take to make our home PCs secure and keep them that way. All PC users should employ the principal countermeasures:

- Install and run anti-virus software (see Chapter 6).
- Set up users with 'standard' user accounts and limit the use of Administrator accounts (see Chapter 2).
- Ensure you are running a firewall (see Chapter 4).
- Choose and use good passwords (see Chapter 3).
- Back up the files you don't want to lose (see Chapter 3).
- Keep software up to date, especially the operating system and internet browser, so that you have the latest security fixes (see Chapter 3).
- Be aware of possible risks and be alert for new threats (see Chapter 3).

Some security measures take no time at all. They are just sensible ways of working that are no more time-consuming than any other. Some security software is freely available and extremely effective. Some security software has a cost as well as a benefit. Chapter 6 will discuss the pros and cons of some of this security software and help you decide which might be most suitable for you according to your risk assessment. The following chapters give the details of what can be done. This chapter has looked at risks in general. Chapter 2 gives an overview of more specific insecurity issues with home PCs so that we understand the relevance of the countermeasures set out in the chapters that follow it.

2　HOME COMPUTER INSECURITY

The good news is that a lot of people in a large and growing industry are working extremely hard to make the security of IT systems better. The bad news is that many devious and criminal people are trying to exploit the weaknesses that do exist. Computer security, usually referred to as information security, is a contest between these two groups. It is a game of 'catch-up'. It is also like an 'arms race'. The bad guys find a way to defeat security, the good guys find a way to fix it. The good guys find ways to improve security, the bad guys find more ways to break it and so on.

As in the real world, there is no such thing as absolute security. Nothing is 100 per cent secure and I make no apology for repeating this. Often, because of the high technology that is involved, this common sense view seems to be forgotten. What this means is that we are never secure, and although we can achieve a good degree of security we can never be complacent. We must take measures to protect what we value and we must continuously monitor our security level.

This chapter goes into a bit of the background of the internet, why it is insecure and what security really means for users of home computers.

INTERNET INSECURITY

The puzzling question about the internet is why is this amazing technological leap forward insecure? Why is it costing organisations millions of pounds to use internet technology securely? Surely it would have been better to have made sure it was secure from the beginning? Well, yes probably! Unfortunately, it's not that easy to go backwards and try to correct some of the mistakes of the past. Even if we could wave a magic technology wand, we might make new mistakes that stop the internet from being so powerful and effective, or stop the PC from becoming so widespread. The original designers had no idea that their technology would become so prevalent, nor did they know that hacking and computer crime in general would be such a problem, so we have to deal with the technology we have today.

The internet
The irony is that the internet emerged from defence research in the 1960s, and the defence community is one of the biggest advocates and implementers of computer security. Somehow the internet, as a research technology, slipped beneath the radar and began multiplying in academia without the sort of security the military might have wished. It does have one key property that attracted the military to it in the

first place and which helped it grow into the size it is today – resilience. If one part of the internet 'dies' the remainder can carry on operating. If the computer that disappeared was delivering email to recipients, for example, then that job can simply be transferred to another computer on the internet.

On the other hand computers can 'join' the internet easily too. In fact whole networks of computers can join. There is no central control. The internet has evolved into a massive worldwide network of networks. If there were some form of central control, this ability to develop and its dynamism might disappear. There is no central internet authority, no contract between organisations, no formal agreement between the participating computers. The only requirement is that they all communicate and interoperate using the same set of protocols. This is called the internet protocol suite (sometimes referred to as IP). Perhaps in the future the internet may become a more stable and secure environment, but until then every user has to take some responsibility for security.

Internet Protocol
Internet Protocol (IP) is a way of sending information between computers. Every device, which is part of the internet, has an IP address. This consists of four numbers (between 0 and 255) separated by dots (e.g. 212.58.244.69). Humans are not very good at remembering long numbers (and in any case these numbers can change over time), so we would much rather use memorable words (such as www.bbc.co.uk for the address (or Uniform Resource Locator; URL) of the BBC website in the UK). When we type this into our browser, the browser accesses a directory service known as a Domain Name Server to find the numeric address of the website. All bona fide human-readable internet addresses can be converted to their numerical counterpart.

Information is sent between computers connected to the internet in chunks known as packets. Each packet consists of data, such as text or graphics, along with a source IP address (the address of the sender) and a destination IP address. Basically the internet works by computers passing these packets around until they reach a computer connected to the destination address. They can then deliver the packet to it. It is what is known as a packet switched network. A packet can be anything, from part of a web page to an entire email. The process is not as random as it sounds. Some internet connected devices have an understanding of their 'neighbourhood', a sort of address book, and so the packets can take an efficient, if not necessarily the most efficient, route to their destination.

The reason that email (and indeed all web traffic unless it is encrypted) is not private is that it is likely to pass through many different systems en route to the intended recipient. It is rather unfortunate that most email systems show an icon that looks like an envelope to represent the command to send an email. In reality, emails are more like postcards in that their contents are not hidden. This a cause of much of the insecurity we find on the internet today.

If you're curious about the route your communications are taking, try this. While online, open a command line interface (this allows you to type commands direct to your computer). To do this, click **Start→Run...** and type **cmd**. At the command line prompt, type **tracert** followed by the web location you want to trace. For example, type **tracert www.bbc.co.uk**. The result is an interesting display of the route that a packet would take, via your ISP, to reach the BBC website in this example. It gives you an idea as to how the internet works.

IP security

IP is the underlying technology of the web. It is a simple mechanism that supports more complex protocols for transporting email, web pages, audio, video and the like. The simplicity is its power but also its security weakness. There is no guarantee that a packet claiming to come from a specific address really came from that address. Any computer can forge packets and thus change the apparent source address. Every packet has to traverse other computers before it reaches its destination. Any computer in the path can, in theory, read, modify or delete packets. There are no restrictions on the type of content in the data section of a packet. Content can be benign or harmful, informative or dull. We cannot trust the packet's origin or its content.

When a PC user starts a web browser, the PC effectively becomes part of the internet and is given its own IP address. This PC is now 'visible' to the internet since it has an IP address and is running some protocol, such as the hypertext transport protocol (http) that provides web browsing. Basically a web browser sends http packets to a web server, using IP. This PC is immediately at risk of probes from criminal hackers. The IP address it is given is purely temporary: the next time the same PC accesses the internet its IP address will be different. In addition, such a PC is only online, typically, for a maximum of a few hours a day. This means there is only a short time window for an attacker to find and penetrate such a system, but it is still possible – the fundamental part of the problem hasn't changed.

A personal firewall is a piece of software you can set up on your PC that 'listens in' as your computer communicates with the internet and monitors traffic. It doesn't read your emails or check out the websites you visit, but it makes sure that only allowed connections, such as email or web browsing, are active. Malicious software typically uses different protocols to set up connections. A personal firewall allows you to ensure that these unsafe protocols are disabled. It can give you some warning if external hackers are trying to use them or are trying to find other holes in your defences. If you have a broadband connection, then a firewall is essential because attempted attacks like this occur frequently.

Whatever we do with the internet, there is some threat, some vulnerability, some risk of a security compromise and an impact on our lives. Each application that uses the internet, such as email and web browsing has to be secured individually. Before we look at these we need to consider the general risks of using an internet-enabled PC.

THE VULNERABLE HOME COMPUTER

If the internet is inherently insecure, then perhaps we can look to technology on the desktop for security. What about our home PC? Unfortunately the home computer, the software we run on it and the way we use it does very little to help us, as we can see by considering some of its components.

The central processing unit

An important part of your computer is the central processing unit (CPU). This comprises a microprocessor, which is the main computing power of a PC. It is responsible for running the programs that you use. A microprocessor is quite discerning in some ways: it only runs machine code that is specially tailored for it. This is the main reason that software for a Mac computer will not run on a PC. However, in other respects the microprocessor is rather indiscriminate. It will run any program that **is** specially tailored for it. It does not care what that program does! It could be a program to delete everything on your hard drive. It could be a program to send all your files to some location on the internet. What a program actually does is of no concern to the microprocessor, but it is of high concern to us. We do not want to run programs that might possibly cause us problems.

The hard disk drive

A further component of the home PC that is relevant to security is the hard disk drive (HDD). The HDD stores all the data you generate when using a PC. Some of this data is in the background, for example temporary or back-up files created and used by the software that the user doesn't normally see. However, all the data is easily visible. A way to secure it is to encrypt all or some of the files. Encryption is a method of scrambling data so that it is unreadable. Data is scrambled and unscrambled using keys. Only those people with the right key can scramble and then unscramble the data.

HDDs can develop faults. These can range from minor faults (e.g. where small parts of the drive become unusable) to major faults (e.g. where the whole drive becomes inaccessible). Valuable data on a hard drive should be backed up and we will see how to do this in Chapter 3.

THE OPERATING SYSTEM

An operating system (OS) is software that makes it easy for application software to use the computer's resources. These resources include the file system on the disk, the presentation on screen and access to any peripherals like printers etc. Operating systems have a critical role in security because they mediate between the files and functions of the PC, and the software applications that use them. In other words the OS is responsible for controlling access to all the data on your PC.

In companies, operating systems such as Microsoft® Windows Vista® for Business, Windows® NT, Windows Server® and UNIX™ are the most prevalent. These operating systems are designed to be used in large networks of computers and have many built-in security features, especially to manage access control for large groups of networked users. Generally, a password is used to allow different users access to their own space with their own files and to ensure these files can only be seen by other users who have been granted the correct permissions.

Most home users have PCs running Windows® XP, Windows Vista® or the newest version Windows® 7. (Some may still use older operating systems, but experts say that they cannot now be made sufficiently secure to be used and should be discarded. I will not be considering them further in this book.)

Logon passwords

A simple, effective and necessary security measure is to make sure all accounts on your PC have good logon passwords.

In Windows® XP: If you are logged in as an Administrator (further details on this are in the section 'Access Control and Windows® User Accounts', go to **Start→Control Panel→User Accounts→Change an account→Create a Password**.

Alternatively, If you are logged in as a Standard User, then perform the following: **Start→Control Panel→User Accounts→Create a Password**.

In Windows Vista®:

Got to **Control Panel→User Accounts→Change your Windows Password**.

In Windows® 7:

Go to **Control Panel→User Accounts→Create a password for your account**.

You will also be invited to provide a password hint. In case you forget the password this may jog your memory, so is a very good idea. For the same reason you can also create a password recovery disk and this will be covered in Chapter 3.

You can always go back later and change this password and in fact it is a good idea to change the password from time to time. This is your login password so it is very important that you do not forget it. Passwords are extremely important so we will look at them in more detail in Chapter 3.

Screen savers

A screen saver can be associated with a password and hence effectively 'lock' your computer to stop other people using it whilst you are away. For it to be effective, the screen saver should appear after a reasonable amount of time. You will probably want to modify this using trial and error. There will be a compromise between the irritation of typing the password in too often on the one hand, and the screen saver not kicking in quickly enough when the PC is left alone on the other. As usual you should also use a risk approach to decide how quickly the screen saver should appear: too slowly will leave the PC at risk so it will depend how often you leave the PC alone and how likely you think someone might attempt to use it without your permission.

The password for a screen saver is the same as your logon password. If you do not have a logon password for your user account you cannot set a screen saver password.

In Windows® XP:

Go to **Control Panel→Display→Screen Saver**. Select a screen saver and then tick **On resume, password protect**.

In Windows Vista®:

Go to **Control Panel→Appearance and Personalisation→Change Screen Saver...** Select a screen saver that you like from the drop-down list, choose a waiting time to suit you and then tick the box that says **On resume, display logon screen** to ensure you have to type your password in once the screen saver has engaged.

In Windows® 7:

Open the screen saver settings by clicking **Start→Control Panel** and in the search box, type **screen saver**, and then click **Set screen saver password**. Tick the **On resume, display logon screen** box and set a time when you want the screen saver to start, then click **OK**.

Access control and Windows® user accounts
Access control refers to managing the capability of different users, and their applications, to access data on a computer.

In order to gain this security, Windows® provides two types of user account, each with different access control privileges: Standard User and Administrator. You should log on to your computer with a Standard User account most of the time. You can surf the internet, send email and use a word processor without an Administrator account. Standard User accounts lack the power of an Administrator account so they are inherently more secure. If a virus or attacker gains access to your account their ability to infect, or affect, the computer is constrained. Unfortunately the default account for most Windows® machines is an Administrator account. Millions of people are browsing the web in a manner that could easily be made more secure.

You need to make sure that all users, including you, are using a Standard User account. An Administrator account should only be used when necessary. You will need to keep one account as an Administrator account, but all general purpose use should be as a logged-in, password protected Standard User.

You can create a new user account whilst logged in as an Administrator as follows:

In Windows Vista® and 7: Click **Start→Control Panel→User Accounts (and Family Safety)→User Accounts.**

Click **Manage another account**. If you are prompted for an Administrator password or confirmation, type the password or provide confirmation.

In Windows® XP: Click **Start→Control Panel→User Accounts→Create a new account** and provide the name for a new account and its password. Note you should ensure it is a Standard User account and not an Administrator account. You can create Standard User accounts for all the users who share the computer. Providing Standard User accounts will prevent users from making changes that affect other users of the computer. It also provides some defence against viruses which may be prevented from assuming the higher power of an Administrator account.

When you are logged on to Windows® with a Standard User account, you can use the computer as you would normally for all your usual activities, but if you want to do something that affects other users of the computer, such as installing software or changing security settings, Windows® will ask you to provide a password for the Administrator account. This security is provided by User Account Control (UAC), a feature in Windows® that can help prevent unauthorised changes to your computer. UAC does this by asking you for permission before making changes that could alter the way your computer operates or that change settings of other users. When UAC is invoked you will see a UAC dialogue box. Read it carefully, and then make sure the name of the action or program that's about to start is one that you intended to start.

In Windows®, when your permission or password is needed to complete a task, UAC will appear with one of the following messages:

Windows needs your permission to continue – A Windows® function or program that can affect other users of this computer needs your permission to start. Check the name of the action to ensure that it's a function or program you want to run.

A program needs your permission to continue – A program that's not part of Windows® needs your permission to start. It has a valid digital signature indicating its name and its publisher, which helps to ensure that the program is what it claims to be. Make sure that this is a program that you intended to run.

An unidentified program wants access to your computer – An unidentified program is one that doesn't have a valid digital signature from its publisher to ensure that the program is what it claims to be. This doesn't necessarily indicate danger, as many older, legitimate programs lack signatures. However, you should use extra caution and only allow this program to run if you obtained it from a trusted source, such as the original CD or a publisher's website.

This program has been blocked – This is a program that your Administrator has specifically blocked from running on your computer. To run this program, you must contact your Administrator and ask to have the program unblocked.

A bona fide UAC message, like those above, is pretty obvious: apart from the dialogue box telling you that Windows® UAC has been activated, the rest of the screen will be fuzzed out. Remember this doesn't mean something is safe. Only if the PC seems to be doing something you instructed it to, or expected it to do, can you be fairly certain it is safe. By this means you can ensure that changes are the ones instigated by you, and not by some unknown piece of software running in the background.

Windows® Safe Mode

Windows® Safe Mode is a very basic Windows® configuration that uses only the most essential services and drivers – just the main programs and files required to run are loaded and some functionality, such as access to the internet, is disabled. This will often allow you to boot a problematic PC and deal with any problems, such as attempting to remove spyware and viruses that may not be removable in a normal boot of the PC. Safe mode is usually the first thing any technician will do when confronted with a PC that will not boot correctly or operate properly, so it is worth remembering this for future reference.

Safe mode is good emergency option to try if you are experiencing problems with your system or if software is causing you problems. It will also help you work out whether the problems you have are hardware or software based. For example, if you can boot in Safe Mode but cannot boot normally, then you have a problem with some software or a device driver installed on your system.

To access Safe Mode, press the F8 key repeatedly about 1–8 seconds after you turn the computer on (just after the initial 'beep' sound that most PCs make when booting up, but before the Windows® logo appears). You will see a menu list of options. Select option **Safe Mode**, or in Windows® 7 on the **Advanced Boot Options** screen, use the arrow keys to highlight the **Safe Mode** option you want, and press the **Enter** key.

Sometimes the only way to remove viruses and spyware correctly is via Safe Mode. Many forms of malicious software will protect or reinstall themselves constantly if they are allowed to start as Windows® boots up in Normal mode. These programs will be included in one of the many 'start-up' locations in Windows®, so when Windows® is started normally, they run as a background process. When you start the PC in Safe Mode, these extra 'start-up' locations are not used. This can allow good virus and spyware removal programs the chance to remove malicious software correctly and completely so that they do not reappear. If you suspect there are virus or spyware problems on your PC, you should always run anti-virus and anti-spyware programs in Safe Mode to ensure that they have maximum effect. If you are following manual virus removal instructions, perhaps to eliminate a specific virus using guidance found on a trusted site on the internet, again you would probably be expected to use Safe Mode.

Another good use of Safe Mode is when applying the System Restore capability. Further details on this are given in Chapter 3. The System Restore utility can be accessed in Safe Mode and used to restore any previous Restore Point:

Go to **Start→All Programs→Accessories→System Tools→System Restore** then follow the instructions to restore your system to an earlier date where you had a previous stable configuration.

Alternatively, at the F8 menu, use the arrow keys to highlight **Last Known Good Configuration** and press the **Enter** key.

To exit from Windows® Safe Mode: Click **Start→Shutdown** and choose **Restart**. This will automatically restart Windows® in Normal mode.

HOME AND AWAY – LAPTOPS AND SMARTPHONES

Laptops are an increasingly popular home computer to complement, or even replace, the traditional PC. Related devices, such as netbooks, and tablet computers, such as the iPad, are convenient machines for casual web browsing and other simple tasks. Portable computers need all the protection measures of home PCs, plus additional protection to cope with the risk that they may be lost or stolen. Perhaps the main way of ensuring laptop security is through physical countermeasures. These include:

- keeping your laptop with you at all times;

- not using a laptop bag to carry it in (which advertises it to potential thieves);

- not leaving it in hotel rooms or out of your sight in any way;

- using a screen guard (these are made from a special material that covers the screen and makes it difficult for people sitting next to you to read what is on your screen).

You can also buy software to help you trace your lost or stolen laptop by reporting its location to you when the rogue user connects it to the internet. This software may also lock data on the device from the new user. If you require further security, then the best option is encryption.

Encryption
There are two main options for encryption on a laptop. You can use the built-in capability of Windows® to encrypt files or folders. This is known as the Encrypted File System (EFS). Alternatively, you can use a piece of software (available in free or paid for variants) to encrypt your entire hard drive. Microsoft®'s BitLocker® is an example of this and is available in Windows® 7 Ultimate, although not in the versions more common on home PCs. Windows® 7 also has the capability to encrypt USB sticks. In EFS, your security is now dependent on your login password, so it is very important it is strong. Similarly, most hard disk encryption tools will encrypt using a password, but this can be different, and much stronger, than your login.

EFS is not available on home versions of Windows®, so you may want to look at the many commercial and free options for either file or whole-drive encryption. There are a number of things to be aware of:

Hard drive encryption can provide a higher level of security than file-based encryption. This is because file encryption is only operating on the file as we see it in its folder. It does not operate on any other copies or versions. These may exist because the software you are using to edit a file has saved back-up versions, or the operating system has left copies in different parts of the disk. Operating systems typically are very messy and when files are being used or loaded from disk they may keep copies somewhere else on the PC just in case they need them later.

Hard drive encryption can be quite complex. For example, you will be encrypting all your applications as well as your data so you need to make sure you have them backed up or have access to them online or on CD. You are also totally relying on the software to work, and totally relying on any passwords you use for decryption. Any mistakes or problems and suddenly all your data is at risk, not just individual encrypted files, so hard disk encryption is not for the faint-hearted. However, if you have any particularly sensitive data, then it requires serious consideration.

Encryption software is also available for USB memory sticks. Sometimes this is included when you buy a memory stick, but is particularly worth thinking about because USB sticks are very easy to lose.

To use EFS and encrypt a file on Windows® XP, Vista® and 7 (but not Home versions), right-click the folder or file you want to encrypt, and then click **Properties**.

Click **General→Advanced** and select the **Encrypt contents to secure data** check box. Click **OK**, and then click **OK** again.

To decrypt a folder or file, right-click the folder or file you want to decrypt, and then click **Properties**.

Click the **General→Advanced** and clear the **Encrypt contents to secure data** check box. Click **OK**, and then click **OK** again.

The first time you encrypt a folder or file, an encryption certificate is automatically created. You need to back up this encryption certificate. If your certificate is lost or corrupted and you don't have a back-up, you won't be able to use the files that you have encrypted.

To back up your EFS certificate, start by opening Certificate Manager. Click the **Start** button and type **certmgr.msc** into the search box, and then press the **Enter** key. In the left pane, select **Personal** and click **Certificates**.

In the right pane, click the certificate that lists **Encrypting File System** under **Intended Purposes**. If there is more than one EFS certificate, you should back up all of them.

Select the **Action** menu, point to **All Tasks**, and then click **Export...**

The Certificate Export Wizard requires to you to click **Next**, and **Yes** to export the private key. Then click **Next→Personal Information Exchange→Next**.

Type the password you want to use for the back-up file, confirm it, and then click **Next**. The export process will create a file to store the certificate. Provide a name and folder for the file and then click **Save**. Click **Next→Finish**.

Store the back-up copy of your EFS certificate in a safe place away from the PC that has the encrypted file.

Using public Wi-Fi points

There are a couple of key vulnerabilities here. Firstly there is a risk in using unsecured networks (i.e. those that are not encrypted). If you have to use an insecure network (and this is usually made clear to you as you connect), then make sure you do not type in any passwords for important websites because these could potentially by detected by an eavesdropping attacker. It is also important to make sure your computer (including a Wi-Fi-enabled smartphone, see 'Smartphone security' below) is not set up to seek and automatically connect to new or unknown Wi-Fi access points. An attacker can set up a 'dummy' access point to mimic a public website, which the PC might have connected to in the past, and may automatically connect to it, exposing it to the attacker. To stop this go to:

In Windows Vista® and 7: **Start→Control Panel→Network and Internet→ Network and Sharing Centre**

You can double-click on any networks listed that are marked as **Automatically connect** and then untick the option that says **Connect automatically when this network is in range**.

This is a little bit more involved in Windows® XP: Click **Start→Control Panel→Network Connections** and then right click the **Wireless Network Connection** icon and select **Properties**. Under the list of **Preferred networks**, select your default and then click **Advanced**. In the dialogue box, select **Access point (infrastructure) networks only** and make sure the box labelled **Automatically connect to non-preferred networks** is not ticked. Click **Close** and **OK**.

This is particularly important for any public Wi-Fi access points that you may have used at places like stations and coffee shops.

Bluetooth®
If you have Bluetooth® on your laptop it is a good idea to turn it off when you are not using it or if you don't use it at all. It can be used as a route to spread viruses or extract data. Thieves can also use Bluetooth® to scan a parked car for hidden phones or laptops.

Smartphone security
What have mobile phones to do with home computer security? Well, for one thing, smartphones with internet access are becoming more like general purpose portable computers that just happen to let you make phone calls. Furthermore, from a risk assessment point of view:

- they may contain important files and data that you don't want to lose;
- they may contain your passwords to certain websites that you use, including those where you use credit cards or PINs;
- they are effectively an additional connection to the internet from a mobile environment, just like laptops;
- they may be compromised, and emails, calls and voicemail hijacked or bugged;
- they may provide access to private sensitive data (e.g. your address, holiday details etc.).

In fact, most of the security measures required for PCs now need to be followed for smartphones. The only difference is that the frequency and impact of the risks is somewhat different and so we need to take care to address the more likely risks.

The main risk from mobile phones stems from a loss of the device itself. Obviously they are easy to lose and the security risk is that the new owner can access your data. This encourages theft. Stolen phones are obviously attractive anyway as a source of free calls for the thief. Many people with contract phones have found large bills run up on stolen phones, so the first countermeasure is a PIN to protect access. However, this might be broken by a determined attacker, and in any event there has been news of vulnerabilities that allow smartphone access despite PIN protection. The main countermeasure is not to store passwords on the phone.

Where possible you need to avoid keeping any sensitive data on your phone. However, this is easier said than done. It may be that you keep your address book and calendar on your phone and this is a very useful feature of modern phones that you don't wish to give up. Similarly, you may access your emails on your phone, and these emails may contain sensitive information. However, don't make a note of passwords, PINs or credit card numbers or account numbers on your phone.

Children may have their own smartphones too and this will give them access to websites and social networking sites, and the accompanying risks. Protecting children online is covered in Chapter 4.

At present, the biggest risk of using smartphones is loss, or theft, so the key countermeasure is to make sure your phone is locked with a PIN or password. This should at least make it more difficult for someone to get access to your personal data. Similarly you should protect your voicemail with a PIN. Obviously you should ensure your data is backed up. Most phones are capable of synchronising with PCs, so it is usually relatively easy for a new smartphone owner to back up their data.

If your phone is lost or stolen, then you should certainly tell your phone company straightaway. The next thing to do is to change passwords on any websites that you access from your phone, and your ISP access and/or email passwords. Typically emails are accessed with a stored password on mobiles and so they are easily accessed by a thief. With access to your email, an attacker may be able to obtain or change passwords on websites that you use. You might also wish to change the password on your home Wi-Fi if your phone is set up to use it. However, the threat of someone using your Wi-Fi via a stolen phone is relatively low and if you have changed the passwords you use then they would have to go to a lot of trouble to cause serious problems.

Some products are now becoming available, for some phones, to delete the data remotely on your phone if it is stolen, perhaps by the sending of a text message. This is something you might wish to consider. Note security products and capabilities will vary from phone to phone, and are changing a lot as the threat evolves. The risks are much the same as for PCs in many ways, so note the following:

- **Avoid illegal downloads** – If you download apps or want to customise your phone with things like ringtones, games or wallpapers, beware of peer-to-peer sharing websites or any websites of dubious legality such as those offering unlimited free downloads. You just can't trust them and so you don't know exactly what you're getting until it is on your phone, and by then it is too late! These sorts of websites are a common route for hackers to infect victims with viruses.

- **Keep your computer virus free** – Your first defence against viruses is to keep your computer's anti-virus software up to date as will be discussed in Chapter 6. If you happen to contract a virus on your phone, the next time you 'sync up' with your computer the anti-virus software should catch the infected file before transferring it. Anti-virus software is also now becoming available for mobile phones and the price/performance of these tools will gradually improve. Eventually it is likely to be as important to have anti-virus software on your phone as on your PC.

- **Turn off Bluetooth® and Wi-Fi** – Keep your Bluetooth® set to **non-discoverable** or **transmission disabled** when you're not using it. There is a risk that a virus can spread via Bluetooth®. An infected phone can scan for vulnerable phones in Bluetooth® range and when it finds a receptive target, copy and transmit itself to the passing phone. Bluetooth® has also been used by thieves to identify whether a parked car contains a hidden phone. Also turn Wi-Fi off when in public. Phones will typically seek out and connect to Wi-Fi networks they think they have seen before. An attacker can set up a 'dummy' access point to mimic a public website that the phone has connected to before and, unbeknownst to the owner, a phone may connect to it and be compromised.

- **Keep your software up-to-date.** A virus could instruct your phone to repeatedly call a number, send your voicemails to a different location or it might destroy your data. Rogue diallers or 'silent callers', for example, may call premium rate numbers. You should keep your software and apps updated just like a PC to ensure any vulnerabilities are patched.

The risks of using mobile phones as portable PCs are rising by the day. Synchronisation and back-up is key, but be aware of new risks and new security tools. Ask yourself the question, if someone had my phone what could they do with it that could hurt me?

SECURING HOME WI-FI

Home Wi-Fi has been such a boon to the use of the internet at home. Many of us now have more than one computer in our house and can access the internet from any room or from the garden. Home Wi-Fi is provided through a broadband router. This is basically a device that converts the IP network traffic communicated over a wireless connection into signals that can be sent and received at high speed over your phone line or cable. Wi-Fi is easy to set up and for some years most computers have been equipped to use it. It should not surprise you to hear that routers can be a source of insecurity to your home network. They are not always set up in a secure manner. In fact they can be insecure 'out-of-the-box' – in other words as soon as they are switched on.

Unfortunately for many users it is not clear how to configure them for security, or to know what actually needs configuring. This leaves a large number of connections susceptible to hacking, where someone can obtain all your internet traffic or use your internet connection, or infiltrate your home PCs. It shouldn't take long to fix any Wi-Fi vulnerabilities you may have, although the exact way to do it will depend on your brand of router. The following guidance shows how to do it for the Orange Livebox. Other modems may have a slightly different interface and different menus that provide the configuration control you require. By reading the following and comparing it carefully you should be able to perform similar actions and obtain the same level of security if you have a different router. If possible, find your router manual or look up on the web for more information from your router manufacturer or broadband provider.

Choose a strong password

Broadband routers typically use passwords to control who can change the various settings. Some of these settings (as we will see below) are security-related, so this password is important from a security point of view. Unfortunately the default password may be weak and the same for every router of that type. Your router may have a default password, in other words it has a pre-set password from the manufacturer. All the same devices will likely have the same password. A hacker can easily find the default password for a router and use it to access the router configuration. You should change it. In any event you should use a strong password. For the Orange Livebox, you can either click on the appropriate icon from when it was installed or point your browser to http://192.127.1.1 (not a typical web address, but see Internet Protocol). This will ask you to log in to your router and, if you have not changed them, you should use the default login 'admin' and default password of 'admin'. Orange recommends these are changed. (For other routers the access login and password should be in your documentation or may be available from your ISP's or router manufacturer's website.) You should now be connected to the Livebox admin pages using your browser. These pages are not coming from the internet but direct from your router. If you now click in the left-hand side on **Configuration** and then **Administrator**, you can type in a new password, retype it and click **Confirm**. Make sure your new password is strong and that you remember it, make a note of it somewhere safe or store it in a password management program (see Chapter 3).

Ensure your level of encryption is high

It is very important to use encryption on your wireless connection. Encryption is the process of scrambling messages or signals in such a way that only the sender and recipient know how to read them. One common Wi-Fi encryption variant is known as Wired Equivalent Privacy (WEP), but it is now considered to be very weak. The alternative is known as Wi-Fi Protected Access (WPA) and this should be used wherever possible. The encryption used depends on a key. This key may be represented as a set of characters like a password, but it should not be confused with the Administrator password mentioned previously. This key is used to perform good encryption. You should ensure that you use a complex key or password. On the Livebox, a long string of letters and numbers is provided as the key. This should provide adequate security as long as you are using it in WPA encryption mode. To check this, log on to the router as before, then click **Configuration→Advanced→Wireless** and one of the WPA options should be selected. If you have WEP security or no security selected, then you have a problem and should try changing it, but you may need to contact your service provider for help. On other routers you need to make sure you are using both a long password or key, and WPA encryption. Bear in mind that if you change the key, or encryption, then the computers that have access to your Wi-Fi will not be able to connect until the new key is also entered on those machines.

Change the default SSID

The Service Set Identifier (SSID) is the name of a router that you see when you search for available wireless networks to connect to. To change yours, log on to the router as before, then click **Configuration→Advanced→Wireless**. You will see **Livebox Name** followed by a box with the SSID. It's a good idea to change the default to something more like a password (i.e. a non-dictionary word or phrase). Again bear in mind that your Wi-Fi devices will need to reconnect to the router using this new SSID.

Other security settings you can control on your router include the firewall. Further details on firewalls are given in Chapter 4, but for now you should make sure it is active by clicking **Security→Firewall**.

SUMMARY

The internet was never designed to be secure. It has evolved to be used for the sorts of activities, such as shopping and banking, which are common today. There is no central control. There is no authority responsible for security. Your security lies in your hands.

- The Internet Protocol is designed to make it easy for the internet to grow and for various forms of communication between its participants to flourish. It was not designed for the commercial activities that have evolved and the security requirements that followed.

- Home computers have a number of intrinsic vulnerabilities. Your need to counter them will depend on the risk assessment made earlier and the specific vulnerabilities on your PC, and the uses you put it to.

- The software on your PC, in the form of the operating system and applications, has to be treated with caution. This includes deciding whether a piece of software is trustworthy enough to be allowed to run.

- All software should be kept up to date with security fixes and should be configured for the maximum security that fits your way of using it.

- Ensure you have good passwords on all accounts and for logging on. See Chapter 3 for how to choose strong passwords.

- Make sure your PC is set up so that you are not using an Administrator account for general day-to-day activities.

- Remember to use Safe Mode if you have problems with the running of your PC.

- Different Wi-Fi routers have different interfaces for user control. You need to configure yours for security but may need to consult your router manual or online help to find out what level of security you are running and how to improve it. Make sure your connection is encrypted with WPA and that you have changed any default passwords.

3   GOOD SECURITY PRACTICE

Information security is not new. Computers have been handling sensitive information and performing critical processing tasks for companies and governments for some decades. Not surprisingly, companies and governments have tried a variety of techniques and technologies to protect their computer-based information. What has been universally agreed is that technology on its own is not a panacea. Good security also relies on good users, good management and good processes. Good users are well-intentioned towards protecting their information.

On the assumption that you are well-intentioned towards your information (or you wouldn't be reading this book) this chapter focuses on helping you become informed about the techniques that information security professionals recognise as good information security practice and shows you how they can be applied on your home PC. Good security practice covers six general purpose activities that should be your closest friends if you want to be secure:

- **Backing up data** – This is the practice of ensuring that data you wish to preserve has been copied and saved so that the copy can be retrieved if the original data is lost or destroyed.

- **Choosing good passwords** – Passwords are the principal access control mechanism we are likely to use. If passwords are guessable, or revealed, then our data is at risk from someone using an account in our name with our password.

- **Patching vulnerabilities** – All software has flaws, some of which may leave security weaknesses in our computers. Software companies release updates, known as patches or service packs, that contain updated versions of software with at least some recently found flaws fixed. These updates need to be 'patched' into your PC to ensure it is secure.

- **Securing your applications** – Applications have power over your machine and, sometimes, your internet connection. If the application decides to do something that compromises security, or rather if an attacker can coerce the application to compromise security, you are in trouble. It is important that you understand the security controls you can deploy from within applications, and ensure that you can trust the applications you are using.

- **Creating a resilient system** – Your home computer can be configured in many ways. Some of these configurations can provide better security through either increasing the barriers to an attacker or decreasing the impact of a compromise. An example mentioned in Chapter 2 is to ensure users only have Standard accounts.

- **Maintaining security awareness** – Security, like everything in computing and technology, is changing rapidly. New threats emerge, new vulnerabilities constantly appear and new countermeasures and security techniques are proposed, developed and implemented. It is necessary to spend some time keeping up to date to ensure appropriate and timely countermeasures can be taken.

BACK UP YOUR DATA

You can tell most software applications to make back-ups on the hard disk and how often to take them. 'Save early and save often' is a useful mantra. However, you may well have lots of other information on your PC that is not automatically backed-up. Does your email software keep back-ups of your emails (both incoming and outgoing)? Do you have a back-up of your Favourites list on your browser? Do you have back-ups of your digital images or MP3 files? Perhaps not. Perhaps you have saved your photos to a CD, DVD or hard disk, but if you delete them from your PC then these back-ups are no longer back-ups but are the only copy, and therefore are at risk. You should consider keeping two copies of any data you wish to keep for the long term.

So this section looks at how we can cope with the more general problem of making back-ups . In other words ensuring that whatever information we have on our hard drive that we do not want to lose is preserved adequately.

Generally speaking back-ups are a chore. That is why they are not performed anything like often enough. This is despite the fact that almost everyone who has ever used a computer has lost data that could have been recovered had back-ups been taken. Back-ups are just like a lot of chores; we do them for a good reason.

There are four key issues to be considered when it comes to performing back-ups :

- What technology to use as back-up storage.
- How often to back up data.
- What data to back up.
- Restoring and testing back-ups.

The trick is to find ways so that back-ups can be done quickly, painlessly and, preferably, automatically. The alternative, losing a lot of data, can be very painful indeed. You have to decide what data you have that you can't afford to lose, and then decide how, and how often, you back it up.

Back-up technologies

Hard disk
Back-ups made by your software applications (such as a word processor) are typically stored on the hard disk just like the original you are working on. Hard drives are not immune to faults. Thus these back-ups are vulnerable to problems with the hard disk. It is always worthwhile keeping back-ups on removable storage media (like CDs) so that there is less reliance on the hard disk. The advantages of

removable media are that they can be stored away from the computer and they can also be used to exchange files. It is not a good idea to back up data to your PC's hard drive. If you need to back up the entire hard disk on a regular basis, then a second hard disk may be required to give you enough storage capacity.

A second hard disk can be internal or external to your PC, although an external one will generally have a slower data transfer rate. Buying a larger capacity hard disk gives you extra storage for data (like photos) as well as for back-ups . An external hard disk can also be portable so that it can be used with several PCs (if you have them) or stored away from the main PC in case of a disaster, such as a fire.

Don't forget that if you back up files to an external disk and later delete them from your PC, perhaps because you have run out of disk space for your photos and movies, then you no longer have a back-up. The external hard disk is now your primary storage and if it fails you have lost all your data. Thus for data you want to store for many years, perhaps much longer than the lifetime of your PC, you should think of storing two copies in different ways. One option would be to store them on an external hard disk and also on web-based storage.

Recordable CD/DVD

Probably the most popular technology for backing up data used to be the recordable CD or, more recently, DVD. There are two types of recordable discs, CD-R (and DVD-R), which can only be recorded on once, and CD-RW (and DVD-RW), which can be erased and reused. For permanent back-ups, CD-Rs are worth considering. They take longer to store data but the fact that they can be written to just once (and therefore the data cannot be overwritten) provides added security. For general regular back-ups , CD-RWs are cheap and versatile. Both types of disc store 600–700 MB of data. Recordable CD drives are available from a number of manufacturers with prices starting at less than £20, and are standard with most new PCs.

The problem with CDs and DVDs is that they now seem to have quite low capacity and they are not as convenient as a USB memory stick for casual back-ups of specific files.

USB devices

A popular storage medium is the solid-state memory stick or thumb drive. These are typically connected to the PC using the USB connection. USB is a way of connecting peripherals, such as printers, cameras and storage devices, to PCs. Many highly portable storage formats, such as USB pens, keys etc. are available. They can be used for back-ups or to copy files between computers. They now typically store much more than a CD or DVD, but less than a hard disk; however, their compactness and portability make them a popular choice. Note they are also easy to lose because of their small size. They are very well suited to short-term back-ups for specific sets of files, but longer term mass back-up and archiving really requires either an additional hard disk and/or storage on the internet.

Web storage

The web provides another possible destination for your back-ups. Free online storage is available from a number of web storage providers. Storage is only one aspect of backing up, so unless you want to back up files manually you will also need some software to schedule and perform the back ups of the required data.

The good news is that there are more and more companies offering these services for basically the price of the storage and this price is coming down. For a few pounds per month you can reliably back up your data to the web.

Back-up storage on the internet has some advantages over other forms of back-up. One is you can access the back-up from any PC connected to the internet, not just from your home PC, so if you think there are files you might need when 'on the road' or on holiday, for example, you can store them on the web for access from an internet cafe. You can also use them to share data as 'public' files with friends and family so they can see, for example, your latest digital photos, your diary or your web bookmarks if you so desire. The other principal advantage is that your data is now well removed from your normal home or office environment. Any catastrophe, such as a fire, that might damage your PC will not affect your data stored on the web.

The principal disadvantage of third-party storage such as this is that there is no guarantee that the company providing the storage will still be around when you want the data back, perhaps in the next year or two, or ten. There is also a risk that your data could be lost by the third party and files corrupted or wiped. For all the reasons we have looked at before you certainly should not store anything like passwords or valuable personal details like credit card numbers, social security numbers etc. Sensitive information must not be sent 'in the clear' to most web drives, and there is a risk if the data is stored on a web server unencrypted. A successful hack of the web server puts all the accounts at risk. It is not advisable to back up any important information on to the web. Neither, as mentioned above, should it be used as the sole means of backing up data that you want to keep for many years. Using it for information you might like to pick up fairly soon or provide for friends is OK as long as that information has little value to an attacker and will not cause you distress if stolen or lost.

If you cannot decide whether or not to use web-based back-up here are a few criteria to help you:

- Is the back-up incremental? In other words, does the software just store the changes you have made since the last back-up?
- How easy is it to restore data?
- Can you configure it to save to local storage as well as online storage?

Some providers will offer a free limited time trial. This is useful because you can see whether there is a significant degradation of the performance of your PC caused by the back-up system.

Frequency of back-ups

One of the first things to decide when planning back-ups is how often to take them. This will depend on how much new data has appeared on your PC and how much old data has been changed in a given time. It will also depend on how valuable this data is to you. In any case, it's worth having a master back-up – take one today if you have not already done so. This master should contain copies of all your most important files and should be stored well away from the computer. With any luck you may never need to use it. From the moment of making a master back-up, all subsequent back-ups need only store the changes since the date of the last back-up.

This is known as an incremental back-up. You have to decide how often to do it. Perhaps weekly, monthly or even daily if you do a lot of work on your PC.

Windows® Backup

Windows® basically gives users the ability to perform two types of back-up:

- **Incremental** – These are back-ups of files onto removable media, where back-ups can be of a specified set of files, selected by type or location on the hard disk.

- **Full** – It is also possible to back up the entire hard drive. In Windows Vista® and 7 you can choose to create a complete back-up and restore image of your PC, which can be used to recover from a hardware failure (using the Back up Computer option in the Back up and Restore Center). This will likely require a second hard drive. To use Windows® Backup on files:

Windows® XP:

The Backup utility is not included with a default installation of Windows® XP Home Edition. However, it is included in the **Valueadd** folder of the Windows® XP Home Edition CD-ROM, so you will need to install this first. The steps to follow are then very similar to those for Windows Vista® and 7 that follow.

Windows Vista®:

Control Panel→System and Maintenance→Back up and Restore Center→Back up files (or Change Settings)

Choose where you want to back up to – hard disk, CD/DVD or removable storage.

If you choose CD or DVD you will be taken through some steps to label, insert and format a disc. You can use multiple discs if necessary, the problem being that you will have to stay by the computer during the back-up process to insert discs as required. If you have the time and inclination to do this, then great, but my preference is to find back-up processes that work with minimal effort so as to make sure they are done regularly. Click **Next**.

Choose file types. Click **Next**.

Schedule – how often and when.

Save Settings and start the back-up, which will inevitably take some minutes. Automatic file back-up will (if scheduled) scan the PC for new files or changed files and save them.

Windows® 7 is very similar:

Control Panel→System and Security→Back up and Restore

If this is your first back-up, then click **Set up Back up** and follow the steps as above, or you can select **Back up now** to create one manually.

If you lose data you can use the Restore function to retrieve data from your back-up:

Control Panel→System and Maintenance→Back up and Restore Center→ Restore files

You can choose to restore files from the latest back-up or from older back-ups (perhaps you need an earlier or original version). You can then select the files and/ or folders to restore.

Which files to back up?

Basically anything that has changed recently should be backed up. If you keep all your data from Microsoft® Word etc. in one place, such as the My Documents folder, creating subfolders as required, then it becomes easy to back up all your Word files just by backing up the one folder.

As well as your precious data, there are other files on your PC worth backing up, for example there are your applications. You may still have the installation CD that they came on or you may not. In the latter case, they are definitely worth backing up. Applications only need to be backed up once. Programs do not change over time (unless they are updated or upgraded), but there are many files that do. Some are files used by Windows® to manage your system configuration and others like your web bookmarks in your browser are saved by the applications. These sorts of files change regularly and thus need to be backed up frequently.

There are three ways to back up your Outlook® email data (stored as .pst files), such as contacts, appointments, notes etc.

- **Personal Folders Backup** – to copy your entire .pst file or files to your hard disk.

- **Export** – to create a file containing Outlook® information, but retain the original data in your folders. You can only export one folder at a time.

- **Archive** – to move the items that you want to retain into separate folders.

The Microsoft® Outlook® Personal Folders Backup tool is available as a download from Microsoft Office Online and is designed for use in Outlook® 2002 and later versions. It allows you to back up Outlook® information to your hard disk.

Alternatively, your emails are stored in folders and are visible to your email client, but as far as Windows® is concerned they are just files in a folder. Microsoft® Outlook Express uses the extension .dbx for its files. The location of the main folder that contains your Outlook Express data varies depending on the version and the location of your Outlook Express program itself. By using Windows® Explorer to look for data files associated with Microsoft® Outlook Express (check for the .mbx, .idx and .dbx extensions in folders associated with Outlook Express (e.g. on my computer they are held in C:\Windows\Application Data\Microsoft\Outlook Express\Mail), you should be able to locate them and then at some point back them up. It is probably worth deleting emails from within Outlook Express if you don't want to keep them, but note that selecting delete just moves the email to the Deleted Items folder and therefore it is still present in the mail store folder we've just located. In order to really delete the email from the PC, both for security reasons and to reduce the size of the mail store folder, we need to delete the email from the Deleted Items folder.

The following shows you how to back up your address book and bookmarked websites:

- Outlook Express Address Book – Go to **File→Export→Address Book...** Select either **Microsoft Exchange Personal Address Book** (which can be imported later) or **Text File** (which can be edited if you need to). Click **Export** to be prompted for a name and a file location.

- **Website bookmarks/favourites** – These can be backed up by saving the whole Favorites folder (C:\Windows\Favorites). If you use Internet Explorer then select **File→Import and Export...** and a Wizard will show you how.

Restoring and testing back-ups

Test back-ups you have taken by attempting to recover the information they are supposed to contain. It is quite possible that the back-up process (especially if it is automated) has gone wrong and the information you require is not being backed up as required. By testing the recovery process you can find out if this is the case now rather than when you actually need the backed up data, which could be too late.

If you haven't taken care of back-ups recently, now is the time!

Data recovery

OK, the worst has happened and you have lost data. Perhaps the back-up didn't work properly (check it next time!), perhaps you deleted work by accident and cleared out the Recycle Bin? Oops! We have all lost data. This section gives a few ways to help you recover lost data.

The first thing to remember is that a deleted file still exists on the hard drive, only that Windows® has been told to 'forget' where it is! The data will survive until it is overwritten, so if you are lucky it may still exist and can be recovered. Use the Recycle Bin (on the desktop), open it and right-click the file and select **Restore**.

There are also commercial files that can help undelete deleted files (e.g. iolo Search and Recover), but remember if the data no longer exists on the hard drive they cannot work.

CHOOSING GOOD PASSWORDS

Passwords are probably the most important security device we all use. They are one of the main ways we gain access to our information. Passwords are also one of the main ways imposters gain access to information. If anyone else discovers your password they will have equal access to your information and equal capability to use that information as you do. There are many ways in which someone can obtain your password:

- By looking at the keyboard as you type it in (so called 'shoulder surfing').

- By guesswork, perhaps by assuming you are using something obvious like your child's name, favourite footballer or pop star.

- By installing some Trojan horse software that monitors the keyboard and tries to detect when you are typing in a password and records it for later sending to a malicious user (known as keylogger software).

- By trying lots of different possible passwords on an account (known as a dictionary attack).

- By obtaining your password over the internet by perhaps faking a website.

- By using an unchanged default password. (When we first start to use a computer system we are sometimes given a start-up password as a default password. These should always be changed at the earliest opportunity because clearly there is a risk that knowledge of this password may be widespread.)

The way a hacker may work is by stealing a password file from a host computer. The passwords in a password file should be held in encrypted form so the hacker still has some work to do. Basically he or she runs the same encryption routine as used by the logon software, against a huge number of possible passwords. When a word is found, which, when encrypted, matches an encrypted password in the password file, the hacker is in. There are software packages available on the internet that have large built-in dictionaries that can be used to rigorously test passwords against a huge dictionary of possible words. Don't be fooled by the word 'dictionary', the guesses will include all words in a standard dictionary, but also other possible words including proper names, two or more words combined, even words from different languages etc. Never use something simple like a name or a place or a dictionary word.

How to choose passwords
The first defence to these types of attacks is to choose a password that is not likely to be guessed or be included in a cracking dictionary. Never choose a password using common names, the names of family members or famous people. It is best not to use a word from the dictionary at all.

A strong password consists of different types of characters: upper and lower case letters, symbols and numbers. The longer the password the more secure it is, but also the harder to remember! Unfortunately choosing a less obvious password means we are more likely to forget it ourselves. The problem is that a password that is easy to remember is often also easy for an attacker to guess. The trouble with strong passwords is us: we cannot remember them. What makes it worse is we may have rather a lot of passwords, for different sites, on our office PCs and at home. We also need to change them regularly for extra security.

More complex password schemes
So how do we choose a good password? The first thing to get right is the length. Most experts would recommend a minimum of eight characters, preferably longer for the most critical data. The longer the password the harder it should be to guess and the longer it would take a dictionary attack to find.

Now let's get some advice from the dictionary attacking programs themselves! One of the companies that produces such software is called 'L0phTcrack'. Look carefully at the word 'L0phTcrack' and you will see it contains several features that make it hard for a dictionary attack to find it:

- It is not a word in the English language (probably not in any language).
- It consists of two words combined: loft (?) and crack.
- It contains a misspelling, 'l0pht' instead of 'loft'.
- It contains a mixture of upper and lower case characters.
- It contains a mixture of letters and numbers.
- It replaces letters with similar looking numbers, that is '0' for 'o' (other possibilities are '1' for 'I', '3' for 'E', '4' for 'A', '6' for 'b', '8' for 'B').

Spaces can be incorporated in passwords to make a pass phrase. Thus we have another way of making a password difficult to guess, but also easier to remember by combining things to make a more complex password scheme, for example:

- **Pass phrase** – Trust no 1, tic tac tow, r0bisc00l.
- **Pass formula** – a=b+c-d; E=mc squared.
- **Pass picture** – (--iii--), ~~~<=//=>~~~

Perhaps you can make use of your hobbies so that your password has some familiarity or memorability.

If you like golf try things like 'birdie the 18th', 'h0le that putt', 'wedge2green'.

If you are into cooking try a 'recipe' like '2oz eggs and milk', or phrases such as 'Frying T0nite', 'D1nner t1me'.

If you know other languages why not put them in the mix? 'Vingt 20 vision', 'Que sera will B'.

But note just using words in other languages is not much more secure than the same in English. Crackers have dictionaries in many languages. Make sure you use punctuation marks and other non-alphanumeric characters if possible.

You can also create new words from the first letter of each word of a phrase or song. For example, 'To be or not to be, that is the question' could be used as a password as 'TBONTBTITQ'. The phrase helps you to remember a word that would be difficult for someone to guess. If you use a phrase or song that's memorable to you, then you will be able to reproduce the password when you need it.

Finally you can encode your password in some way. For example, if you are using a simple password like 'EARLYBIRD', you could make it more secure by swapping each letter for the one that comes after it in the alphabet (i.e. change A to B, B to C etc. to get 'FBSMZCJSE'. No one is going to guess that!) Or swap each letter for one near it on the keyboard (keep it consistent so it is easy to reproduce, e.g. swap each letter with the key to the right on the keyboard).

Another possibility is to use the sorts of abbreviations often used in texting, such as 'Gr8' for 'great'. So use '8' to replace 'ate' or 'ait', '4' to replace 'for', 'u' for 'you' and so on. But make it complex. Just using a simple dictionary word and making these replacements is not likely to be secure.

You can use your imagination and ingenuity to be as original as you like. In fact, the more original the better. Have fun!

Protecting passwords

Sometimes you will forget a password. For a website, a replacement can usually be sent to your email address. Clearly there is a risk to this approach so it is a good idea not to use it unless you really have to, and you should always change any default password. Best practice is for a website to send a weblink by email and this link allows you to reset the password. After a little while this link expires so even if someone got access to your PC they could not use the link to change your password. However, if someone had access to your email (perhaps by stealing your PC) they could request password resets by email for all the accounts you use. So the password that allows you to access your email is probably the most important password you use and should be one of the strongest.

Microsoft® Windows Vista® and 7 also have the capability to set up a password recovery disk, which you can use to reset your Windows® login password if you forget it. In both Windows Vista® and 7, go to **Control Panel→User Accounts and Family Safety→User Accounts→Create a Password Recovery Disk** and follow the instructions. You can use a USB memory stick. A good idea is to use an older one that you rarely use because it only has a small amount of memory. Keep it somewhere very safe.

A further weakness in the password system is that sometimes passwords will be 'remembered' by the PC. A web browser, for example, may suggest that it remembers the password to a website account, or your email program may remember your email account password. There are two ways to address the most sensitive passwords. One is to use a password management program, which we will discuss later in this chapter, to keep your passwords securely encrypted, and thus hidden. Or, if you are worried about forgetting the password, write it down and store it somewhere very secure, such as a safe or locked cabinet, well away from the computer.

Some security advisers hate the thought of writing passwords down, but, carried out sensibly and carefully, it can help security. Indeed, banks acknowledge that people may have to write down their bank card PINs and advise that the PINs are kept secure and away from the card. Some of us with poor or failing memories may certainly need to do it. Even on government classified systems it is sometimes preferable to choose a strong password and write it down, as long as it is stored in a secure cabinet, rather than choose a weak password. However, if you can possibly avoid it, passwords should not be written down. Once you feel confident you have memorised it, destroy the written copy unless you want to make sure it can be accessed by someone you trust, such as your partner.*

It's difficult to remember so many passwords, and the better passwords are the hardest to remember, so to address this trade-off we can select easier passwords

---

*Note that were you to lose your memory, or even die, there could be data locked away that your loved ones need or want access to.

for websites that are less sensitive and harder passwords for websites that must be protected well, like banking. It is risky, however, to have the same password for multiple websites because if one password is found the other websites become open. This happened in 2010 when hackers published passwords taken from a website and it was found that many were very simple but also that people had reused their password on other websites. Thus the original cracking of the passwords led to the attackers having the ability to break in to other websites.

It should now also be clear that passwords are absolutely confidential. You should **never** reveal them to anyone. This is one of the few sacrosanct rules in information security. If you ever have any suspicion that a password has become known then get onto the system and change it.

One last time for luck. Never reveal your passwords to anyone. Thanks for listening.

Password management software
Password management software is a way of keeping many passwords on a computer so that only their rightful owner can see them. How is access to these passwords controlled? Typically, by using another password known as a master password. Thus you only need to remember one password to be reminded of all the others that you use.

Usually such tools scramble or encrypt passwords and save them on your hard disk. The master password is used as the key for unscrambling. The usual advice applies about making sure this password is strong and memorable, but it is even more important now because if it is cracked or compromised all the other passwords become visible. Having a single password is a convenience, but also a vulnerability because it is a single point of failure. Forgetting that one password stops you using all of the others. It is also risky in that it controls access to many places. If your PC was stolen or the hard disk was corrupted you would be unable to get to your passwords until you were able to get a new system and restore your data from a back-up (because of course you will have backed up such important data!).

There are some other advantages of using password management software. Firstly, it might allow you to cut and paste, or drag and drop, passwords directly from their application into the login field. In this way you don't need to type in the password and so it cannot be picked up by a keylogger as described above. Secondly, as you no longer need to remember the passwords you can use much more complex passwords and leave it to the program to remember them for you. Some software will even generate strong passwords or random characters for you. Some of these programs are available for free home use. A widely used free example is KeyPass Password Safe (http://keypass.info) and there are commercial offerings too. Password Safe includes another interesting feature whereby you can use a 'key file' instead of, or in addition to, a master password. The key file is basically a master password in a file and you can keep that file on a USB stick or somewhere safe and use that to gain access to your password list. Note that if you lose the key file or it becomes corrupted, it is just like forgetting your master password and you will lose access to your password list.

An alternative approach can be used for website access: a master password is stored on a server and provides a single sign-on to many websites, saving you the trouble of remembering lots of different passwords. Usually you will have to register and provide information about yourself, and so the 'holder' of the master password controls what information about you is released to which sites. This means you can be placing considerable trust in the holder. Examples include OpenID, GoogleID, YahooID and Windows LiveID, which each give access to a specific set of sites without the need to re-enter the password. It is therefore imperative that you should have a secure password if you use these services.

I am off now to change my passwords!

PATCHING VULNERABILITIES

A modern PC contains a great deal of complex software. Complex software can be a security risk in two ways. Firstly, it can operate in ways in which the original designers didn't anticipate or test. In some instances these modes of operation can have security consequences. Secondly, no software is perfect: it all has bugs of some sort. Some bugs can have security implications. Hackers find out about vulnerabilities due to these software flaws and learn how to exploit them. In order to protect our PC from these vulnerabilities we need to ensure that our software has as few flaws as possible. The way we do this is to get updates from the software vendor. Usually these are free. Upgrading a piece of software to fix a security vulnerability is known as a 'patch'. Most software vendors release patches as part of an update. If we take steps to download theses updates and patches we can protect ourselves against a large number of hacking threats.

Patch management is an important security process. Although patches can be extremely important there is a cost in terms of the time it takes to download, install and reboot to deploy a patch. There is also the risk that the modification causes problems in other parts of the system. Not all patches are created equal. Security sensitive software, such as the operating system, anti-virus and personal firewalls, need regularly updating to keep ahead of the attackers who are trying to find ways around them. Software that accesses the internet is also a risk, so browser and email programs must be patched. Other software, unrelated to security or the internet, is less important but should certainly not be ignored.

Windows® update
It is particularly important to ensure that the Windows® operating system is patched regularly. As we have seen, the Windows® operating system is critical to the security of your PC and any security vulnerabilities that are found in it are likely to be exploited by the hacker community. To keep Windows® as secure as possible use Microsoft®'s Windows® update service at http://windowsupdate.microsoft.com. This checks for available updates to system files, device drivers, service packs and new Windows® features. It will suggest any important updates that should be made to your system configuration. You may also find that a series of updates are integrated into what are known as service packs. These may contain a large collection of bug fixes and enhancements. Bear in mind that they may be megabytes in size, so you will need time to download them.

Windows® variants have a service life. That is to say after a certain amount of time they are no longer supported by Microsoft® and the necessary security fixes and patches are not available. At this point you will need to ensure you have supported versions or Services Packs or else you will need to upgrade to a new version of Windows®. For example, Windows® XP Service Pack 2 ended on 13 July 2010 and no security updates are now produced by Microsoft®. Similarly, on 12 July 2011 security updates ceased for Windows Vista® Service Pack 1. It is important to check what version of XP, Vista or Windows 7 you are running:

To check your Windows® version and service pack:

Click the **Start** button and in the **Run...** box type **winver**. This will produce the About Windows window with your Windows® product name (such as Vista Home, XP Professional or the like). If you look carefully, you will also see the version number (referred to as a build number) with the service pack number.

For future reference the Microsoft® website http://windows.microsoft.com gives details of any versions of Windows® that are no longer supported. However, as long as you have Windows® update running you should find out if your version is at risk.

To use Windows® Update:

In Windows® XP, select **Start→Control Panel→Security Center** and make sure **Automatic updates** is on.

In Windows Vista®, select **Start→Control Panel→Security→Windows Update**

In Windows® 7, select **Start→All Programs→Windows Update**

This will show any outstanding update or gives you the option to Check for Updates, which will compare the catalogue of Windows® patches and upgrades against what is actually running on your PC. You are then given the option to review and install updates. The important part here for security is the section entitled Critical Updates and Service Packs. Unless you have a good reason to decide otherwise you should install everything in this section.

The other important option is Change Settings. This gives you further options, but the most important is to select **Install Important Updates Automatically (recommended)**. You should also tick the box under Microsoft Update to ensure your Microsoft® products, such as Word and Excel®, are updated in the same manner. Note you can select the time and frequency that updates are installed and this should be done on a daily basis.

In Windows® XP, select **Start**, then right-click **My Computer**, select **Properties** and the **Automatic Updates** tab. This will give you a set of options:

- Turn off automatic updates [not recommended].
- Notify when updates are available.
- Download updates but do not install.
- Automatically download recommended updates and install them.

If you select the automated option, you can also select the time and frequency for your PC to check for updates.

Windows® 7 has a new feature known as the Action Center that provides a centralised location for notifications relating to security:

Control Panel→System and Security→Action Center

It consolidates notifications about security issues so you can ensure you are prepared and up to date in the following areas:

- Security messages
    - o Windows® update;
    - o internet security settings;
    - o network firewall;
    - o spyware and related protection;
    - o User Account Control (UAC);
    - o virus protection;
- Maintenance messages
    - o Windows® Backup;
    - o Windows® troubleshooting;
    - o check for updates.

CREATING A RESILIENT SYSTEM

Most software on a PC can be customised by the user in some way, for example the toolbars or default settings, such as colours, fonts etc. can be set up to suit individual preferences. Some settings on software can have security implications. In other words they may have certain weak settings that provide vulnerabilities that might be exploited by an attacker. The biggest risk here is software that has some interaction with the internet, such as email and browser applications, but the operating system, on which most applications rely, can also be vulnerable to attack. In order to reduce the risk from such vulnerabilities we try to ensure that any settings or options are set as tight as possible. This approach is often referred to as security hardening or clampdown. It allows us to create a more resilient system.

Security clampdown

There can be a small price to be paid for clampdown. Some features of software may have inherent security risks, but, on the other hand, they may be extremely useful. If we turn them off we may not get the full benefit of the software we are using, so we have to use our judgement of risk to decide how tightly we should clamp down software. This applies to all our software: email, browsers, operating system and other applications. In some cases we may play safe, for example if a particular feature is little used, then we may turn it off. On the other hand, unless we know there is a specific risk, we may choose to keep a useful feature switched on.

It is very difficult to decide exactly what to clamp down. As well as using our risk assessment, which we discussed in Chapter 1, we have to be aware in case any new threats and vulnerabilities emerge. Computer security is a fast changing business and new threats, vulnerabilities and countermeasures are continually arriving. The next section will suggest ways for you to keep up to date and recognise when new security actions are required.

Note that it is not only the operating system and internet software that can have security vulnerabilities. We will see later in this chapter how macros in word-processing software can be run automatically and used by malicious software to spread viruses or to attack our data. In effect we also have to clamp down Microsoft® Word.

Sometimes software, malicious or otherwise, may corrupt certain system files and there are risks involved with tampering with these files when trying to recover normal operation. Fortunately there are various tools that can help perform activities such as repairing the Windows® Registry if necessary (not to be undertaken lightly), but it is also possible to take your PC back in time to a point before the system was corrupted. This is known as setting a system Restore Point.

System restore

Windows® XP, Vista® and 7 come with a useful feature for troubleshooting software problems, known as System Restore. If you have just installed new software and found that your PC now refuses to boot, you are experiencing some problems that you think might be due to malicious software, or you are suddenly experiencing lots of crashes, then System Restore may be the answer. System Restore creates a Restore Point every time you install new drivers or software. If there is a problem on your system, you can roll your system configuration back to the pre-installation state at the Restore Point where the system worked correctly.

Using the System Restore feature on Windows® PCs is not to be confused with restoring from a back-up. System Restore only restores system files, not any data managed by you the user. System Restore regularly creates and saves Restore Points, which contain system information, such as Registry settings. You can also set Restore Points manually using **Control Panel→System→System Protection**, then click **Create**. This is a good idea if you are going to download software, especially software that might make use of or alter your system settings (e.g. security software).

If you have problems and want to go back to a Restore Point, then:

Select **Start→All Programs→Accessories→System Tools→System Restore**

Or **Control Panel→System and Maintenance→System→System Protection**

Now select your preferred Restore Point. You can also use the above menu options to set a Restore Point.

For added virus protection you could do this in Safe Mode, but if a System Restore is performed in Safe Mode it cannot be undone.

Disposing of your computer

Deleting your data is not enough. As we have seen, deleting a file does not actually remove its contents from the hard drive, it just stops Windows® programs from seeing it. The same is true if you try to format the entire disk. For practical purposes the data cannot be seen or used but with the right tools an attacker can retrieve it. That means any private information, credit card numbers or the like, could be recovered. If you have no further use of your PC, then do not just get rid of it or sell it as is. You must ensure the hard disk contains no data. There are two ways to do this. One is to physically destroy the platter, which is the disk component of the drive that stores the data. Physical destruction means breaking it into bits carefully in a safe way. You will probably need to remove the drive from the PC before doing this. Then remove the platter from the drive. Of course this makes the drive unusable and thus the PC itself pretty useless. Alternatively, there are free software programs available that do a complete secure erase of your hard disk. An internet search should point you to something that suits you. Obviously a complete delete will remove the Windows® operating system, so a new owner will have to install it again.

In any event, think carefully before disposing of your PC.

SECURING YOUR APPLICATIONS

All computers need applications, like email or word-processing, to make them useful. Application software performs the functions that we want to use the computer for. In a sense, the utility of the computer is defined by the applications it runs. As with the operating system, application software should be kept up to date and, where possible, clamped down.

Applications range from games to office productivity tools, from email clients to web servers, from utilities to programming language systems. Every application has to be considered a security risk. Many seemingly innocuous pieces of software may try to access the internet for updates or even to report back on what they are doing. The problem is if they are found to have flaws then they could be exploited by hackers. The simplest answer is to limit the number of applications on your machine. If you don't need it, then don't install it. If you no longer need it, then uninstall it. If you are not sure what it is, then leave it alone unless you think it might be a piece of malicious software, in which case you will need to remove it.

Go to **Start→Control Panel→Add or Remove Programs** to safely delete an application. There may also be an 'uninstall' command next to the name of the program in the list of programs obtainable from the Start button.

Some words of warning: it can be risky to delete application files directly without going through the correct uninstall program as described. There is the possibility that some files are used by other applications or you accidentally delete files required by the operating system itself. This could render your system seriously defunct.

From a security point of view there are five things we need to consider when deciding whether to download and use new application software:

- **Does the software come from a reliable source?** – There is a lot of software available on the web. Some software is packaged and originates from a large company. Some may be illegally distributed online, breaching copyright. Some can be packaged to look authentic, but are actually pirated products. There is no guarantee of the source of any piece of software you buy or download. Software from an unreliable source may not function exactly as it appears. It might contain malicious code that runs invisibly whilst it is doing its expected functions, or it might be malicious in its own right.

  Without verifying the origin of a piece of software we cannot know if there are risks. Buying packaged software from a high-street retailer is likely to be problem-free. Downloading a pirate copy (so called 'warez') of software, or running software obtained from an obscure website, is likely to be risky.

  Some software may arrive at your PC claiming to be 'signed' and implying this makes it more trustworthy. 'Signing' of code, or of messages in general, is an accepted and generally safe way of providing extra confidence in authenticity. It is implemented using encryption techniques that we will learn more about in Chapter 5. For now it is worth noting that, as with every security technique, there are ways around it, but if a website is using signed code it does at least give an indication that they recognise that what they are doing (providing you with software) is risky for you (not them!) and are giving you a little extra information to help you decide whether to trust them.

  A special note here concerns hacker software. There is a lot of software available that automates some of what hackers try to do. On the one hand, the hacker-authors of such tools might not want to irritate their hacking chums by putting malicious code in them. On the other hand, some hackers might feel that there is poetic justice in putting malicious code into software that will be used by people with little knowledge of programming or hacking. If you are ever tempted to use hacking tools at least remember that no one (of a trustworthy disposition) can vouchsafe them for you. Just say no!

- **Does the software do what it claims to do?** – Do not be fooled by a piece of software having a benign name. A 'screen saver', for example, sounds intrinsically safe. The name suggests that it is software that displays images on the screen to hide what you might be working on from prying eyes and to protect the screen if the display is unchanged for a long period. What harm is there in that? Maybe none, but a screen saver is just another application. Any application you run on your computer has the power to do whatever it likes with your system. That's why you should only run software you trust. The PC has no way of distinguishing a screen saver from any other program. It could be benign or it could be hostile. Be wary of software. Be extremely wary of software sent to you, or swapped or exchanged informally. You should ensure that any software you use comes from a reputable and reliable source. Remember it is impossible to ensure that software does only what it claims to do.

- **Does the software have any security-related bugs or flaws?** – All software has bugs. A bug is a programming error that causes a software malfunction. Software also has flaws. These are situations where the software works as expected, but there are also unwanted side effects. Bugs and flaws are facts of life. The more complex the software, the more likely it will have bugs and flaws. And software is getting more complex.

Some bugs just effect the operation of the software. A minority of bugs have security implications, called vulnerabilities. These might range from exposing passwords to leaving open back doors into systems or making it easier for viruses to propagate etc. Generally speaking, reputable software companies will publish fixes, known as 'patches', as they discover new vulnerabilities.

The developer has fixed the problem and released the patch, but the vulnerability doesn't go away until the modified software is installed on your machine. How to patch and update your software is covered in more detail earlier in this chapter. An example is the Service Pack 2 (SP2) release for Windows® XP users, which Microsoft® released, and which fixed a number of security holes.

It is worth noting that the availability of upgrades and bug fixes is another good indication of the trustworthiness of a website. If a website has software for download but appears to have no upgrades or bug fixes you are either downloading a very early version (risky in its own right) or the organisation does not care about the weaknesses of its product.

- **Does the software interact safely with other applications?** – Many modern applications get their power from their ability to interact with other applications. Your browser automatically starts other applications, for example 'viewers' for certain types of web data. Many office applications can run 'macros' written in a computer language such as Microsoft® Visual Basic®. They make use of the Visual Basic® library to get their power. These macros are small programs that perform some function designed to improve the capability of the host application. This sort of connectivity is often quite complex and the results of unplanned interactions can be difficult to predict. Hackers often exploit weaknesses that emerge in this way.

- **Can the software be customised to reduce the security risk?** – Many applications, especially modern office applications and those that use the internet, have a range of options to control their operation. These controls can often be tailored to provide a desired degree of security. The software that is particularly risky, and therefore should be carefully constrained, is any that sets up connections to the internet. Software does this in a variety of ways so you will need to consult the manual or help files for your particular application.

Downloading files
How do we go about downloading? First of all be careful! Check that the software you are about to download is the correct software, the correct version, for the correct machine. Create a new folder to download the software into so that you do not accidentally overwrite any existing files. Make a note of this folder name or create it in the Desktop so you can find it easily (see later).

If you have any applications running, then it is a good idea to close them down. It is a particularly good idea to close down the application you are patching or downloading. At the very least make sure you have saved all your work from any applications you have open. It is quite common for downloads to cause PCs to crash, so save first. You have been warned!

If you are upgrading a full program you can make a back-up of the old software by copying everything in the directory that houses the application into a new folder. In that way, if the download fails or the new software does not work properly on your machine, then you can recover to a state that you knew worked beforehand. You can also make use of System Restore discussed earlier. The backed-up application does not need to be kept forever. If the new version is giving good service, then you can delete the old copy later if you are running out of disk space.

Now click on the download to start the process. You are usually given the option to **Open the file** or **Save to disk**. You can play it safe and save downloads to disk first. The download is more likely to fail if you try to combine the two steps of saving and running the program. You can keep a little more control of the process by keeping the two stages separate.

You will probably be asked where you want to save the file. Choose the folder you created earlier (see above). This is probably the stage where a lot of novice (and experienced) downloaders go wrong. Unless you know the destination of your download you will be potentially wasting a lot of time trying to find it. Quite often though, the application will suggest a sensible location.

Read the instructions carefully. Patches may need to be downloaded directly into the folder that contains the application being patched. The browser, however, may try to put it somewhere else. Perhaps a folder that ends in /temp. If this is the case, the specific instructions for that software should take precedence. Read any prompts carefully. Dialogue boxes that say things like **Do you want to overwrite an existing copy?** might provoke the answer 'no' if you have forgotten to back up.

When the download is finished, open the folder (remember, you made a note of it!). If the file is a .exe file, then double-click to run it. Follow any software-specific instructions. If the file is not a .exe, then you should have had instructions as to what to do. If you are still unsure, then there will usually be a file labelled 'README' that offers help.

In the next section, as an example, we look at security in one of the most widespread applications: Microsoft® Word.

Securing Microsoft® Word

Probably one of the most commonly used applications (apart from the web browser) is Microsoft®'s word processor, Word. Word gives quite a few options for internal control that have relevance to security. These options have similar mechanisms in related programs, such as Microsoft® Excel®, and in software from other vendors, so we can use Word as an example of how to control applications.

Firstly, Word has the ability to make back-up copies of your word-processed files whilst you are working on them. Note that Word uses the file extension .wbk for previous versions of a document file (which have the file extensions .doc or .docx). You may need to know this if you want to recover older versions in case of problems.

In versions earlier than Word 2007, go to **Tools→Options...→Save**. Click the boxes alongside **Always create back up copy**, **Allow background saves**. In Word 2007 and later, similar options can be found by clicking the **Office button** (at the bottom of the menu that appears when you click the **Office button** at the top-left of the Word window) and selecting **Word Options→Save**. Then tick **Save**

AutoRecover info every:. This last box then requires a time to be entered. This is the time interval between back-up saves. If it is too frequent it can be annoying, but if you are a fast typist you do not want to risk losing too much. A time of somewhere between 15 to 30 minutes is probably appropriate. You will also need to specify a folder where back-ups are to be saved to. In Word 2007 and later, this location is just below **Save AutoRecover information...**. In earlier versions, go into **Tools→Options...→File Locations** and select **AutoRecover files**. If no folder is listed or you want to change the one that is, then click the **Modify...** button. Browse your folder structure in the window that appears, to find or create a folder in which to store the AutoRecover files. Click **OK** twice to complete the operation.

Protecting documents

Word also provides a level of access control over its documents using passwords. You can either force a password to be required in order to view the document or to modify it. Note that this access control is not absolute. Word will block access to the file, but the file is still visible to other applications that understand the Word document format. Simple editors that look at the individual characters can also be used to find the text in a file although they will not produce a visual copy of the file in the same way as Word. However, you can use this control to block files from novice computer users, but anyone with some computing prowess who wanted to read or modify the file could probably do so.

In Word 2007 or later, this feature can be found by clicking **Protect Document** on the **Review** ribbon.

In Word versions earlier than Word 2007, you can protect documents from viewing or editing by going to **Tools→Options...→Security**. If you want to stop anyone else from looking at it in Word, type a password under **Password to open:** and if you just want to stop it being modified, type a password under **Password to modify:**.

Word (and other office applications) also has a feature to control the use of macros. Macros are a type of program, but because they can be hidden inside files like documents and spreadsheets, they are often used to conceal malicious code and to propagate viruses. If you have received a file from an unknown or dubious source, then you should be wary before loading it and be extremely cautious before letting any macros run. Fortunately we can configure Word to warn us if macros are present. When a file containing a macro is loaded into Word a warning gives you the option of enabling or disabling them. If you disable them, you should avoid any risk; however, the file may not appear correctly on the screen or function correctly.

Word 2007 and later versions control the use of macros through the **Word Options** button. You can then click **Trust Center→Trust Center Settings...**, although the recommendation is to leave the default protection in place. Similar macro control can be found for Word versions earlier than 2007 by going to **Tools→Macro→Security...**

I have mentioned before that software complexity can often result in security weaknesses. The Microsoft® Works suite, which is the reduced functionality office software from Microsoft®, for example, does not have the capability to run macros and is therefore immune to macro viruses. However, increased security is balanced against reduced functionality. The Works spreadsheet program cannot read spreadsheets generated with Excel® unless Excel® saves them in a specific format. Microsoft® Office applications are considerably more powerful than their corresponding Works applications. This is an example of how the software business (and its customers) tends to favour functionality above security. Until security is demanded by consumers as a priority, the increasing complexity of software will continue to expose security vulnerabilities.

STAYING AWARE

The whole point of this book is to help you become aware of the risks of information security and what you can do about it. Awareness of the risks of information security is extremely important and has to pervade all your use of the PC. You have to have a healthy suspicion in order to be secure. For one thing, security needs to be understood by all the users of your PC – your whole family if necessary. In professional security circles the phrase 'information security is everyone's responsibility' is sacrosanct. The weakest link in security is people, that is we, the users. We make mistakes, we take risks knowingly or unknowingly. If you just blindly trust everything that happens, you could be accepting serious risks, so beyond the risks we have discussed so far what else do we need to be aware of?

Social engineering

One aspect of information security that is completely about people is referred to as social engineering. Social engineering is the art of influencing the actions of others through social interaction. In the non-computer world we know it as subterfuge, disguise and deceit. Someone pretending to have come to read your electricity meter but who in reality is looking for something to steal is performing social engineering to get into your home. The basic premise of a social engineering attack is plausibility. If you believe that they are who they claim to be, and are doing what you would expect that person to be doing, you will, generally speaking, place some trust in them and cooperate with them.

Even security has been used as a pretext to dupe a user. Scareware, for example, covered in Chapter 6, can advertise fake anti-virus software, pop-ups, even phone calls saying you have a virus and offering to help. Some criminal gangs have set up call centres to do this and get their software onto peoples' machines where it can steal credit card and bank account details.

A typical example in information security is someone trying to trick you into giving away your password. A 'social engineering' attack like this uses the fact that most people do not realise that they should keep passwords as secret as their cash machine PIN. Many people have been duped by a plausible email requesting that they provide their password. The email may purport to come from a shop or bank that they have recently had some dealing with. This provides the plausibility. How would anyone but the shop or bank know that they had just had this transaction with the bank? Well it could be someone on the inside who knows it as part of their job, or it could be a hacker who has found out through other means. You certainly cannot trust the origin of emails. The social-engineered email follows this up with a statement to the effect that the shop or bank computer operations had a fault and lost some customer details, and that if you could provide your password then everything could be put back to normal. The request is so plausible many people blithely send their passwords. Only those who have the awareness never to reveal their passwords are likely to be resistant to this approach. And this is one of the simplest social engineering attacks.

More recently, a social engineering scam followed an announcement from the UK tax office that many tax payers were due a refund. Many people received bogus emails requesting bank details and personal information. These emails did not come from the tax office who stated that they would never contact anyone they owed money to in such a way.

Awareness is important when it comes to repelling social engineering, but there is another factor that can be used to your advantage: suspicion. You should retain a healthy level of suspicion over what happens on your PC. A social-engineering attack relies on you not questioning what is happening. There are many other occasions when you should be suspicious:

- **Unusual behaviour by your programs** – Perhaps the most worrying would be unexpected attempts to connect to the internet (but note that many applications do this quite legitimately).

- **The claims of security product vendors** – Especially those that claim to be foolproof or 100 per cent secure (or as one I saw recently claimed, 101 per cent secure!).

- **If you receive unexpected email from someone you do not know**.

- **If you receive any email containing software to be run** – Never double-click on email attachments as they may be malicious programs or disguised to look like ordinary application files such as from Word or Excel®.

- **Any requests of any form for information that should be kept private** – Passwords, social security numbers, bank account details, credit card numbers etc.

File sharing software

As we have seen, whenever your information is made accessible or available on the internet, either through email or over the web, then, because of vulnerabilities in operating systems etc., there is a risk. It should come as no surprise that software designed for sharing files, usually known as peer-to-peer sharing, over the internet is inherently risky.

The original file sharing program to gain a large user base was known as Napster. This allowed users to advertise that they had MP3 music files available for others to download. MP3 files are compressed digital music files, and if someone got hold of your MP3 files by accident or without your agreement you might not be too upset. However, more modern file sharing programs can share any type of file. What's more, if they are not configured carefully, it is possible that all your files could be made visible to other users of the file sharing software. Your accounts details, your correspondence, digital photos etc. could be exposed. You, personally, may not have downloaded this software and have no interest in it, but can you be sure your children haven't? It's worth (a) talking to them and (b) checking your system for any programs that could be file sharing software. These include Gnotella, BearShare, Gnutella, Morpheus and others. I am not saying that any of these programs are bad, but this type of software is inherently risky. You need to know if they are on your PC, and, if you want to use them, you need to make sure that they are tightly controlled so only the barest minimum number of files are shared.

A related category of software is known as remote control software. These programs allow a user to control a 'host' PC on which the software is installed from another PC on the internet. Again there are obvious risks here. An intruder might find a way to defeat the security controls in the software (e.g. a password) and thus have complete control over your computer. Remote Access Trojans (RATs), discussed in Chapter 6, work in exactly this way.

Websites and online articles

Get Safe Online is a UK government and industry programme that has recognised that home and small business users find it difficult to get the right information about security, and are confused about what they should do. Their website is at www.getsafeonline.org. Two other useful online resources are: www.safekids.com and www.saferinternet.org. www.v3.co.uk gives news and features on viruses and virus issues, and anti-virus advice.

Keeping up to date

Another reason that awareness is so important is that the risks change over time: attackers find new ways to attack, new vulnerabilities are found in applications and operating systems. It is necessary to keep up to date with these events. The web is probably the best way of staying in touch with what's happening in information security. A list of useful websites is provided at the front of the book. Get Safe Online also operates the ITsafe Warning Service, which provides online timely updates about security issues from UK Government sources. To get early warning of new risks, the professional information security community have Computer Emergency Response Teams (CERTs). It is worth your while checking regularly with a CERT – a good website is www.cert.org. Another website worth watching is www.securityfocus.com. Microsoft® provides a newsletter on security for home computer users at www.microsoft.com/protect/resources/newsletter.aspx.

Vulnerability scanners

Finally, in spite of our best attempts to keep our home computers secure, we are bound to miss something or something might change that leaves us vulnerable even if we think we have already addressed it. To counter these problems, professional security people bring in outsiders to check up on security. These checks can take the form of audits (in which the security process is discussed), penetration tests (in which a mock attack is performed) or vulnerability checks (in which software is run remotely to test whether any holes or back doors have been left open, or whether any software is out of date and has security vulnerabilities).

Bringing in outside experts for an audit or penetration test is too costly for a home user but a remote vulnerability check is feasible. There are free checks available from well-known suppliers on the internet. Do beware, however! The techniques used by vulnerability checkers are very similar to what hackers would do to find out the weak points of your system. However, you want to find out your vulnerabilities before the hackers do, so you can fix them. Find a trustworthy source and run a suitable set of checks. Here are some examples:

- Shields-Up! is a well-respected service run by the Gibson Research Corporation at www.grc.com. This scan helps to check the security of your system and particularly the robustness of your firewall.

- Symantec are one of the largest security companies and offer Security Scan which covers a range of tests.

- Audit My PC have a range of online checks: www.auditmypc.com/freescan/prescan.asp

But beware hoaxes! Remember, you are giving an online scanner access to your PC, so you need to be certain you can trust it. Check out any information you can about it on the internet. Look for feedback and positive reports about it from multiple sources. Also do not confuse vulnerability scanning with virus scanning. Most virus scanners or anti-virus programs run on your PC, but some of the above scanners also perform some anti-virus checks over the internet. A well-worn attack of late is to convince users by email or through a dodgy website that they have or may have a virus on their PC. Often the user is asked to run a scan of their system. This will inevitably find a piece of malware, probably fictitious. They are then charged money to remove this bogus problem. This is known as 'scareware'. Do not be coerced or invited into scans. Research, review and choose a reputable company.

SUMMARY

- Backing up your data is absolutely critical. Decide how you are going to do it and how often. Store back-ups away from your PC. Test your ability to restore from the back-ups.

- Passwords are the principal way to protect information and you need to practise devising and remembering secure passwords. Choose passwords with mixtures of letters and numbers (and other characters). Never use words in dictionaries, people's names or place names. Do not write passwords down unless they are kept securely in a wallet or safe. **Never** reveal your password to anyone. Change passwords regularly or if you believe they may have been exposed.

- All software will have bugs that can make them vulnerable to security compromise. Check regularly for software patches for your applications and operating system. Make sure Windows® update is on.

- Some systems may be vulnerable and patches may not be available. Look out for advice on plugging security holes and harden your system accordingly.

- Stay aware of developments in home computer security and check vendor sites for news about possible vulnerabilities and patches for your operating system and application software.

- Be suspicious. Security is not fixed solely by technological means. We, as users, play a key role in protecting our systems from social engineering, con artists and scams. Finally, as an aide-memoire about passwords, remember this adage: Passwords are like underwear: don't share them; don't discuss them in public; don't leave them dangling from your monitor or stuffed under your keyboard; above all change them regularly!

4 SECURITY ON THE WORLD WIDE WEB

Chapter 3 presented a range of security countermeasures. Each of these measures is helpful against a range of security threats and contributes to an overall security posture. As we discussed in Chapter 1, the extent to which we need these measures depends on how much risk we want to take with our computer activities.

A computer that stands alone, unconnected to any network, can be a very secure computer. It is much more difficult for an attacker to breach, and easier for the user to control what happens to it than a computer on a network. Before the extensive introduction of business networks and public networks like the internet, information security risks were far more manageable. Connecting to the internet, running applications over the internet and doing business over the internet put our computers and information at risk. The most common internet applications are email (see Chapter 5) and surfing the web.

SAFER SURFING

Surfing, or web browsing, is actually a very safe activity. Millions of people surf for hours every day with few or no security problems. Unfortunately this comfortable picture of safe surfing hides the fact that web browsing does have inherent risks and it lulls us into a false sense of security. The risk of an information security incident whilst you are surfing is low, but the impact, if something were to happen, might be high if, for example, you were using your credit card or banking online. This risk assessment suggests that if surfing is something you enjoy, then take a few basic measures, some technical and some non-technical, and take particular care where the potential impact is high.

Basic precautions
The main risks in normal every day browsing occur when we go to a new or obscure website. Most of the large commercial websites take security very seriously and their web pages will not be intentionally or accidentally malicious. This may not be true of some other websites, particularly those with content of a dubious nature, and you are best advised to steer well clear. Some browser vulnerabilities have allowed a website to read any file on your PC or write to your PC. There is also the risk that you download something that you think is harmless but in fact is a malicious program.

Protected Mode
Microsoft® Internet Explorer®, versions 7 (not XP), 8 and 9, operate by default in 'Protected Mode'. You should make sure this is switched on, confirmation should

be visible at the bottom-right of the browser window. This mode runs the browser in what is known as a 'sandbox' (a sort of compartment that the browser can not break out of). In Protected Mode, Internet Explorer® has no capability to send files to the rest of the operating system. The idea is that these restricted privileges make it much more difficult for an attack that attempts to use the browser to write, alter or delete data, or install malicious software.

Using security zones

Not all websites are created equal. Some can cause us problems. Internet Explorer® has a feature known as security zones to tailor security settings according to our belief in the trustworthiness of the website. Internet Explorer® allows you to classify websites into four zones: the Trusted zone, the Internet zone, the Restricted zone and the Local intranet zone. Each zone comprises a group of security settings that control what the browser and the web pages you browse can do.

The Local intranet zone is irrelevant unless you have a home network. All websites are automatically in the Internet zone unless you specify otherwise. If you trust a particular website you can put it into the Trusted zone, and if you do not trust a website you can put it into the Restricted zone. You can set the security level for each of the three zones: strongest for the Restricted zone and weakest for the Trusted zone. Security settings for each zone can be customised or left at their default settings.

Assigning a website to a zone

To put a website into a security zone in Internet Explorer®, go to **Tools→Internet Options→Security***

Select the zone you wish to add the website to. (Note that you cannot add sites to the Internet zone because all websites are in it unless you transfer them to a different zone.)

Click the **Add Sites...** or **Sites** button.

Check or type the internet address of the website you are adding to the zone in the box marked **Add this website to the zone:** (note this does not apply to the Local intranet zone).

Click **Add**. Click **OK**. Click **OK** again.

Setting zone security controls

You now need to decide which settings to apply and whether to accept the default settings that are low for trusted sites, high for restricted sites and medium for internet sites. My advice is to make the Internet zone as tightly controlled as you can bear, but to change only the default settings if you are confident in what you are doing (especially if you are reducing the security level). As you disable features you will get more prompts and more error message from websites that are trying to use certain risky features. It becomes rather irritating to keep dealing with the dialogue boxes

---

*You will be using the Tools menu items a lot, so it is worth remembering that Tools are represented by a picture of a cog on the Toolbar. ⚙ Tools ▾

that appear. Some features occur on almost every website and every web page, so getting frequent prompts can be extremely irritating, but it can be pointless from a security point of view because we just get into the habit of saying 'yes' to the prompt. You can balance a high level of Internet zone security by putting your most visited websites (assuming they are bona fide and worthy of trust) into the Trusted zone.

You should consider what the various features do and what risk they may expose you to before following some recommendations on customising the zones. This will help you make the decision about what to enable or disable. Ultimately this is down to you, but you should always try to be aware of when to increase the security of a zone, for example if a certain feature becomes more risky than previously realised or if there is a general increase in concern over web surfing.

There are two main issues to address in your internet security configuration: how much to control software and how to manage your privacy. Software comes in three forms:

- **Standard executables** (usually labelled as .exe files) – These can contain any sort of program. Most software and software upgrades are downloaded in the form of .exe executable files. One way to run such code is to select **Run** from the **Start** menu and type in the name of the program. As we have discussed before, running unknown software can be very risky.

- **Component software** – Generally in one of two forms: ActiveX® and Java®. These are usually small pieces of code used to add some particular feature to a web page, such as a graphic. They are generally constrained by what they can do on your PC so are less powerful than standard executables, but they can be downloaded and run without your knowledge.

- **Web page scripts**, such as JavaScript® and Visual Basic® scripts (VBS). What scripting languages can do on your PC is tightly constrained, so they are generally the safest of the three types of code. However, they can also be run without your knowledge as you browse the web.

So ActiveX®, Java® and web scripts can be run without our knowledge, but we can configure the security zones to warn us or to stop them running. ActiveX® is more risky than Java® because it can get access to all of your PC just like a standard executable. Java® is run inside a 'sandbox', which restricts its access to your PC. To add security to ActiveX®, a developer of an ActiveX® component can 'sign' it to show its origin. Signed code is likely to be safer than unsigned code because it give us the possibility of identifying the originator.

Web page scripts are pretty safe and should be enabled unless you can put up with interminable prompts (almost every web page uses scripts). Be wary, though, because the situation could change. A bug in a piece of software, coupled with a malicious script from a dishonest website could change this from low risk to high risk. The only way to know this is to keep aware of the current security situation, as we discussed in Chapter 3.

Some recommendations are:

- At a minimum your internet security zone configuration should prompt for all activities related to ActiveX® except for 'Download unsigned ActiveX controls' and

'Initialise and script ActiveX controls not marked as safe for scripting', which should be set to Disable. All ActiveX® settings should be disabled in the Restricted zone.

- In the Internet zone, Java® should be set to high safety, and should be disabled in the Restricted zone. 'Scripting of Java applets' and 'Active scripting' can be enabled in the Internet zone.

Internet Explorer® allows you to choose a default security level for each zone or you can customise the security of each zone using a menu. To set the security level of a zone: Go to **Tools→Internet Options→Security**.

Select the zone you wish to consider changing the security settings of. Click the security level you wish to apply. For the Internet zone it may be worth considering a customised setting by clicking **Custom level (expert users only)** – see further details below about how to customise the zone. Do not be too worried that it says expert users only. You can always reset the level back to low, medium or high if you are in any way unsure about the settings you have chosen. You do not want to make your security too weak, so choose to disable features, or request prompts to allow something to happen, rather than enable features. It is not a good idea to set the your level on the slider lower than the default.

Common alternative applications

The most widely used applications on home PCs are Microsoft® Word, Internet Explorer® and Outlook®. They are frequently targeted by malicious software and by hackers because of their ubiquity. One way of avoiding this is to use one of the alternatives and set them as the default. You will be asked whether you want this when they first run. Examples include:

- Alternative browsers: for example, Google Chrome, Apple Safari, Opera and Mozilla Firefox.
- Alternative email packages: for example Eudora or web-based email, such as Gmail and Hotmail.
- Alternative office suites: for example Google Docs or OpenOffice.

No one can claim with absolute confidence that any of these programmes are intrinsically more secure than their Microsoft® equivalent. Some security professionals use them and would claim that they are exposed to fewer problems because of it. Each of these applications still requires configuration in much the same way as the Microsoft® applications. As they all operate slightly differently it is not possible to go through all the security configuration issues here, but by using the examples given for Internet Explorer® and Outlook Express®, it should be possible for you to find the equivalent controls in these applications.

One of the major factors in deciding whether to adopt these alternatives is the amount of time required to install the new system, test it and then move data from the Microsoft® applications to the new ones. A replacement email package will need to import your existing email directories, address book and other preferences. A replacement browser will need your 'favourites' list as well as your security options.

Responding to security warnings

Whenever you are prompted to take a security decision (e.g. whether to allow an ActiveX® control), you must make some judgement about whether the activity is likely to be safe. You can make this judgement (a risk assessment) based on four factors:

- **The nature of the website** – Do you trust it? Have you been there before? Is there a reason why it is requesting this permission?

- **General risk situation** – Are there any relevant security alerts on the internet? Are you running an unpatched browser?

- **Specific risk situation** – Are you currently doing something sensitive, such as using a credit card?

- **Suspicion** – Is it possible that you are being attacked, harassed, targeted or under some form of surveillance?

Never get into the habit of mindlessly clicking OK to security warnings – if you do, then you might as well switch them off because they are providing no effective security.

FIREWALL THE INTERNET

A firewall is a gateway between networks or computers connected to a network (such as the internet), blocking unwanted data that attempts to pass through it. The reasons a firewall is important are twofold. Firstly, they can protect you against unauthorised outbound traffic. There may be software on your PC that unbeknownst to you is trying to communicate over the internet. Examples include viruses and worms trying to spread, and spyware trying to relay information back to base to report on your browsing, buying or listening habits, or your personal details. A good firewall will detect this and allow you to stop it. Secondly, firewalls can stop unauthorised inbound connections. Hackers will attempt to scan your computer to see if you have any vulnerable programs or operating system features that they could use to attack your system. A good firewall will detect these scans and block them.

A firewall can be thought of as a traffic light that monitors all the traffic (data) and decides whether it is benign (green light – the data is permitted to pass), is potentially harmful (red light) or requires some form of checking (amber light). As we have seen, networks can 'talk' using many different protocols. Some protocols are more vulnerable to attack than others and hence might be disallowed by the firewall. Other protocols might only be permitted with machines with specific addresses that are known to be benign or friendly. In businesses, firewalls run on dedicated computers and hence can act as a buffer zone between the internet and an internal network. A dedicated computer is not really a viable option for the home user but a personal firewall is an alternative.

A personal firewall is a piece of software on your PC that 'listens in' as your computer communicates with the internet and monitors traffic, usually, and preferably, in both directions. It allows you to ensure that unsafe protocols are disabled. It can give you some warning if external hackers are trying to use them or are trying to find other holes in your defences.

A firewall is an essential piece of armour for your internet security. The good news is for all the currently supported versions of Microsoft® Windows® an internet firewall is included as standard and by default is switched on. However, it is worth checking that yours is definitely on. To do this:

In Windows® XP: Click **Start→Control Panel→Network and Internet Connections→Network Connections**, then right-click the connection you wish to secure. Click **Properties** and then click the **Advanced** tab. Then in **Internet Connection Sharing** tick the box marked **Protect my computer and network by limiting access to this computer from the internet**. Click **OK** to finish. (Please note that this might not be exactly the same on your computer.)

In Windows Vista®: Click **Start→Control Panel→Security** and under the heading **Windows Firewall** click **Turn Windows Firewall On or Off**. You can then check it is switched on (and switch it on if necessary) in the next screen.

In Windows® 7: Click **Start→Control Panel** and in the search box type **firewall**. Click **Windows Firewall** and in the left pane click on **Turn Windows Firewall On or Off**. You can click **Turn on Windows Firewall** under each network location that you want to protect, and then click **OK**.

There are also other software firewall programs that can be downloaded. You need to ensure that if you have enabled a new firewall, then you turn the Windows® firewall off. This is because having two firewalls running can cause problems, especially if they disagree about whether to let traffic through. Of course, only turn the Windows® firewall off when you are happy with your new firewall and it has been turned on.

SECURE E-COMMERCE

E-commerce is the term for using the web for commercial transactions like buying, selling, auctions, trading and banking. When surfing the web there are particular activities that are riskier than others. It is only common sense to see that anything of a financial nature, such as shopping or trading, is likely to be more risky, perhaps because the impact of a mistake is bigger or due to malicious intent. One famous bank robber replied when asked why he robbed banks: 'Because that's where the money is.' Criminals will target financial transactions on the web. Security in e-commerce is therefore very important.

It is not recommended to do financial transactions on a public PC; however, if you do use a publicly accessible, or otherwise shared, computer for web browsing, such as in a library or internet cafe, when you have finished the session you should clear out the temporary files and history list (see later in this chapter). If possible, reboot the PC. Make sure no one is watching if you type in something sensitive like a password.

Confident web shopping
Basic precautions

You should always take a few simple precautions when shopping on the internet. Firstly, use well-known and respected companies wherever possible. If you cannot be sure of the credibility of the organisation from their website give them a phone call and check them out. Any reputable company will provide a physical address and phone number on their website. Be particularly careful if buying from abroad. It may be difficult to clear up any problems and their legal system may not be sufficiently developed to allow redress if necessary. Secondly, always use a credit card when making payments over the web. In most countries there is a maximum amount (of around £50 or $50) that you can lose as a result of fraudulent use of your credit card (internet or otherwise). Thirdly, always print out a copy of the offer and order, keep a record of the web address and any email or other contact addresses and phone numbers.

Some websites will display so-called 'seals of approval' such as TRUSTe and Which? Webtrader. These are schemes where an independent third party has checked that the website is operating to certain standards. Websites that are part of the scheme display a picture of the seal and a link to the website of the seal organisers. The standards vary from scheme to scheme so it is difficult to know exactly whether it is relevant to your particular transaction unless you click on the seal. This lets you find out what the seal signifies and also to verify that the website is a bona fide member of the seal. A fraudulent website could just show a picture of the seal with no real link to the seal owners – such websites must be avoided.

Websites can be taken over. Some hackers will deface a website, a bit like graffiti on a wall, just to make a point. Skilled and determined criminals could potentially get inside a website and monitor it. Alternatively, they could set up a dummy site that looks like the website you were expecting, but it is really under their control. This means that when you enter your payment details they are not going to the merchant you want to deal with but to a criminal interloper.

Can you trust what you read on the web? You can trust any information if you trust the source. In the case of the web the source is a website, so the real question is: can you trust what appears to be coming from a website? Unfortunately there are various ways in which an attacker could divert your web browser to a different website. If you thought you could trust that website you might submit a password, credit card or account details to it without realising that in fact it was a fake website controlled by an attacker. The substitution of websites like this is known as 'web spoofing'. Attacks like this have occurred frequently on the internet. The attacker sends out an official looking email claiming to be from a large commercial company. The email contains an apparent link to the company's website. This is known as 'phishing'. Closer inspection shows it is not the correct address of the company but perhaps something very similar. The fraudster sends out many emails hoping to ensnare at least some people who are unaware of the type of attack or who do not check things carefully enough. A version of this attack has taken place with apparent links to the PayPal website. PayPal is a widely used payment service that acts as an intermediary for payments across the internet. Fraudsters have sent out emails with a legitimate looking PayPal logo that links to a PayPal-like website. Users log in as if it were the real PayPal website and if they divulge any financial information it is picked up by the fraudsters. The real PayPal website is not involved in any way.

The main precaution you can take is not to click on links if you are in any way suspicious of them. In addition, before you click on a link, hold the mouse cursor over it and check that the status line displays the URL (website address) you expect to see, that it is accurately spelled and matches the name of the organisation. Some links are text descriptions, such as 'MegaPCShop', and when you pass the cursor over them you can see their web address at the bottom of the browser window. Now an attacker could put up a web page (or send you an HTML email) that had 'MegaPCShop' on the page but actually directed your browser to a completely different website. If that website were made to resemble the real MegaPCShop website you might be duped into providing your credit card details. As explained in the section 'Internet Protocol' in Chapter 2, Domain Name Servers convert the website address into an IP address for that website. Domain Name Servers can be taken over by attackers, but they are carefully defended by professionals. The risk to a home user is when you see an IP address, such as 123.231.321.321 and click on it, you have no idea where you are heading.

If you put favoured websites into the Trusted zone, then, if they are spoofed, the spoofed website will be in the Internet zone, and if you have set the zones up accordingly you should get some warnings of the website running Java® or ActiveX® (most websites, whether spoofed or not, will use them) that you would not get if it was the real website in the Trusted zone. This should make you highly suspicious.

Secure transactions

You have heeded the above advice and are taking precautions about who you do business with, and you want to enter into a secure transaction. What do you do? Basically you need a secure way to send your credit card and order information across the internet so that only you and the business can read it. For that you need to encrypt the transaction. There are many possible ways to do this, but the most tried and tested (and hence trusted) way is known as Secure Sockets Layer (SSL). Any other method should be treated with caution. All reputable businesses use SSL via a website address prefixed by https rather than just http.

SSL works using what is known as a digital certificate. A digital certificate is a digital identity and an associated key. The identity has been verified by the issuer of the certificate (a so-called trusted third party) and the key is used to encrypt any information sent. Anyone presenting a digital certificate is stating who they are and providing you with a key that allows you to send them information securely. They (and only they) have the complementary key that decrypts the information. Thus a secure transaction can be performed. This process happens behind the scenes automatically when we use a web browser to undertake a secure transaction, but there are things we can do to check the process is running properly:

- The browser should show a dialogue box to confirm that you are now accessing a secure website. If so, you can safely click OK.

- The website address should appear in the address bar as **https**://www... rather than the usual http://www..., where https is an indicator of the secure http protocol.

- A small image of a locked padlock is shown to the right of the address bar in Internet Explorer®.

- Check the digital certificate of the vendor by going into **Properties→File** where you can see information about SSL, then click **Certificates** to see the certificate information. This should be issued to the same organisation you are doing the transaction with and you should also check it is within its dates of validity.

- Only provide financial information just as you make a purchase and always provide the minimum amount of information.

SSL only provides point-to-point encryption, from you to the website. It does not tell you whether the vendor is trustworthy, what country's laws they abide by, that they keep customer information secure, that their privacy policy is acceptable or that they will even follow it. Just because a website uses SSL doesn't necessarily make it a good website to do business with. It is necessary, but not sufficient.

Avoiding frauds and scams

Many scams arrive by email and are the electronic versions of long-standing fraudulent schemes. The UK's Department of Trade and Industry and the US Federal Trade Commission published a list of the 'Top Ten Dot Cons' (www.ftc.gov/opa/2000/10/topten.shtm). Don't get caught out by the following scams:

- **Internet auction fraud** – Goods bought in an internet auction are either wrongly described or don't even exist and never arrive.

- **Internet Service Provider scams** – Cheques were sent to people, but on cashing them they found that they had effectively agreed to the sender acting as their ISP and suddenly found their bank accounts were being debited every month with fees that were difficult to get stopped.

- **Web cramming** – Small businesses were offered free web pages and then found themselves billed for pages they didn't know they had.

- **Adult websites** – Users of adult websites who gave out credit card details found themselves billed for services they had not ordered or authorised. Many may have been too embarrassed to complain.

- **Business opportunities** – These tend to offer high earnings for limited effort and are long on promises but short on detail. One of the most common is work-at-home schemes.

- **Pyramid selling** – Where you pay a small amount to someone higher up the chain and attempt to 'sell' the benefits of the pyramid (and subscriptions) to more members below you. (Also chain letters.)

- **Investment opportunities** – These usually offer surprisingly high, and ultimately unachievable, rates of interest on your money. They may attempt to appear as novel investments (in recent years ostrich farming was a common ruse!) or they may be the so-called Ponzi schemes where initial investors are effectively paid interest from the deposits of newer investors, thus encouraging them to believe the scheme works so they invest more and recruit new investors. Ultimately, of course, the new money is insufficient to continue the scheme and many people lose out. These schemes may also claim to be risk-free or offer guaranteed returns. Don't believe a word of it! Be particularly cautious of any scheme suggesting an 'offshore' investment – this may seem like something sophisticated but in reality it means more risk.

- **Prizes and lottery winnings** – These state they you have won a prize (guaranteed) and that if you send some money you could win big. They are usually unregulated systems and your chances of winning anything are negligible. They may promise you a prize from a set of prizes (which sounds good, but often the prize has conditions attached) or a free holiday (where only the accommodation is free as long as you pay for a flight and pay over the odds for food in advance). A variant on this scheme is a request from someone in a developing world country who needs your help to extract his millions from a corrupt state. The person requests your bank details in order to transfer the money out of the country. Once the person has your details he or she makes a transfer – unfortunately this is more likely to be a transfer out of your account and into theirs!

- **Telephone frauds using premium rate numbers** – This covers various scams where people are duped into phoning or faxing premium rate phone numbers set up by the fraudster.

- **Health frauds** – These range from the selling of bogus diet products, unproven cures and untested herbal remedies to incredible cosmetic body work.

If you've come across a website that is offering suspiciously good deals, you need to:

- ask yourself whether the website is selling a quality brand at too cheap a price – is it an offer that is too good to be true?
- check where the website is registered, how long it has been registered and to whom it is registered – you can search for domain name registrant information using an online search tool, such as www.whois.com or www.nominet.org.uk (for .uk domain names);
- always check for feedback, both positive and negative – type the website name or business name into a search engine;
- find out about the company you're buying from and where it is based by using a search engine – companies should supply their full geographic address, not just a post office box or mailbox number;
- find out how to contact the company and look for a landline number – check the number works or whether it is just an automated message or answerphone (be wary if only an email address or mobile phone number is provided);
- beware of companies that have recently set up and have a tiny or non-existent internet footprint.

If it looks too good to be true, it probably is.

Banking on the web

If you do banking over the web it should already be clear that this is potentially a high-risk activity and therefore you should be ensuring that your PC and your internet activities are as secure as possible using the techniques and technologies recommended in this book. There is no magic bullet for secure web banking. Probably the most critical security activity for web banking is in choosing and protecting your password and account details. As discussed previously, it is vitally important to choose a strong password – your e-banking password should be your strongest. All other advice relating to passwords should also be followed: never give it out to anyone, don't write it down, don't send it across the internet and change it regularly. If you really must write it down, do not leave it near your PC or next to your account number: store it securely and make sure that it is not recognisable as an e-banking number. Avoid using publicly accessible PCs for e-banking.

So passwords are the biggest target for cybercriminals. Even a strong password can be obtained by criminals using a spoofed bank website or a keylogger on your PC recording your typing.

Some of the bigger banks these days provide additional hardware-based security devices, but this does not mean that the security measures in this book can be ignored. No security measure is 100 per cent effective.

An online banking survey in late 2009 found that more than a third of people in the UK do not use online banking because of security fears. The study, conducted by industry analyst firm Gartner, found that 38 per cent of British consumers and 41 per cent in the USA listed security as the most important reason they do not use online banking. Earlier, the FBI released a warning to consumers in the USA after revealing that a total of $100 million (£60.5 million) had been stolen through online banking fraud in the country.

Before conducting banking on the web it is worthwhile to ensure that the reputation of your bank is high. Use a well-known name, but if you need or want to bank with a smaller or unknown bank then do some background research to check them out. How long have they been around? Has anyone on the internet had any particularly good or bad experiences with them? Whenever you undertake a transaction try to keep a paper record of what happened – just in case.

All websites that you interact with should have a privacy statement. This can be a quite long-winded statement and although it is advisable to read all of it, in practice it is time-consuming and only worth pursuing in key circumstances. Banking online is a case when it is worthwhile to read your bank's privacy statement. Find out how they handle information about you, whether you can find out what they hold and whether they will delete it once you cease to be a customer.

Avoiding phishing scams

The above advice should keep you in good stead with the increase in so-called phishing scams. As we have mentioned previously, these are one of the most dangerous and clever deceptions circulating on the internet. A phishing scam arrives as an email, which purports to be from a bank or other commercial website, that requests information from you about your account. This is an attempt to trick you into disclosing details that can be used to access your account. A phishing email may ask you to login and verify, update or change your details (sometimes they have the cheek to suggest this is for security reasons!). The emails may appear extremely plausible and they usually provide a link to a website. The deception is that the website is a fake and is designed to look exactly like your bank's website. If you type in your account details these will be captured and used to steal from your account at a later time.

So far, customers do not seem to have been held liable for money extracted from their accounts in this way and the banks have taken the loss. They generally do this for credit card fraud too, which impacts a much greater number of people for large sums of money. However, it is clearly in all our interests to avoid these frauds and even if your loss was made good there could have been a period of time in which you were caused significant embarrassment or had difficulty with cash flow.

Internet Explorer® version 7 has a control to provide a warning of a possible phishing site: **Tools→Internet Options→Advanced**. Then scroll down to **Phishing Filter** and click **Turn on Automatic Website Checking**.

Internet Explorer® versions 8 and 9 have a feature known as the SmartScreen Filter. This includes a set of tools for:

- **phishing protection** – To screen threats from 'imposter' websites seeking to acquire personal information particularly passwords;

- **application reputation** – To remove unnecessary warnings for well-known files, and show severe warnings for high-risk downloads;

- **anti-malware protection** – To help bar potentially harmful software from your computer.

To turn it on go to **Safety→SmartScreen Filter→Turn On Smart Screen Filter**.

Be careful, if the filter is already on, then the option will be to turn it off, which you don't want to do.

The banking community have set up a website to help customers and to provide a one-stop shop for advice on e-banking security. This is at www.banksafeonline.org. uk. The following key measures should be kept in mind:

- Be suspicious of any emails that ask for your personal details. Do not click on any weblinks in such emails. They are often cleverly disguised to look like bona fide links to your bank's website, but in fact they link to the fraudster's website.

- Check your bank's website and www.banksafeonline.org.uk for news and advice on security.

- Check your bank statement for abnormalities.

- Keep your PC secure and keep your passwords and account details private.

- It is usually safe to type the address of your bank's website directly into the browser window if you want to access your bank. Do not give out private or banking details over the internet unless you are certain you are on a secure website that you have accessed directly.

PROTECTING CHILDREN IN CYBERSPACE

Internet safety
The internet can be a dangerous place for children. They may not seem to be in immediate direct physical danger, but there is psychological danger and certainly risks that could lead them into physically dangerous situations. The internet can also be a fun and educational place for children. Internet information sources put a world of knowledge at their fingertips. Communication by email, social networking and instant messaging can keep them in touch with friends and relatives.

Children are spending increasingly more hours a week online. Many of them know more about the internet than their parents, and use different software and systems, so it becomes difficult for parents to know how to look after their children in the online world.

As ever with information security, there is no magic bullet to solve these problems. The most widespread and relevant technology to protect children online is known as content control or filtering. This software works in a variety of ways. Some types scan incoming email and web pages for pornography, profanity and the like; others check web addresses against a list of websites known to have inappropriate content.

Browsers can be configured to screen out certain websites that provide a self-classification of their content. This is not 100 per cent effective and sometimes it can even be overprotective so that children try to find ways around it. The Content Advisor filtering available in Internet Explorer® is described later in this chapter. Some ISPs offer a filtering service, which attempts to prevent inappropriate material from being viewed. All such filtering can only partially address the problems. Technology is one part of the solution. Good parenting is the other.

Obviously the type of care exercised over children will depend on their ages. Younger children will not resent a parent looking over their shoulders, neither will they try (too hard) to subvert any protection measures a parent might install. Older children, beginning to assert their independence, will be different, and just as children have to be guided through the moral maze outside cyberspace in order to become responsible and happy citizens, they also need guidance through the issues raised by cyberspace.

According to the Internet Watch Foundation (www.iwf.org.uk), which investigates and monitors offensive websites, there are three areas of potential danger to children: contact, content and commerce.

- **Contact** – Children should be repeatedly reminded not to give out personal information on the web: especially addresses and phone numbers. They should also be made aware that the people they meet online are not necessarily who or what they claim to be. It is, in effect, the same issue as not accepting sweets from strangers.

- **Content** – You should check for inappropriate content by viewing their browsing history. You can also look for any files that children may have downloaded, such as images in .jpg or .gif format, or movies in .mpg or .avi format. Go to **Start** and **Search** for files with those file extensions. You can view them all at once by right-clicking in the search window and selecting **View→Thumbnails**.

- **Commerce** – Children should always ask before undertaking any commercial transaction and should never use a credit card without explicit permission.

Windows Parental Control

Windows Parental Control provides some extremely useful features to manage children's use of a PC.

In Windows Vista® Home: Go to **Start→Control Panel→User accounts→Setup Parental Control**.

In Windows® 7: Go to **Start→Control Panel→User accounts and Family Safety→Setup Parental Controls for any user**.

Each user you wish to control should have a Standard user account and you will need to have an Administrator account. If you haven't set up your PC like this then you need to do it now. See Chapter 2.

Then under Parental Controls, click **On** to enforce current settings. You can now adjust the following settings:

- Time limits – when children are allowed to log on to the computer.
- Access to games – to choose age-rating levels and to decide whether to allow or block unrated or specific games.
- Allow or block specific programs.

In Windows Vista® you can also switch on some website filtering when you are setting the parental control by clicking **Windows Vista Web Filter→Block some websites or content→Block web content automatically** and selecting the content level you want.

In Windows® 7, web restrictions and activity reports aren't included in Parental Controls. You can still restrict the websites your children can visit and see reports of their online activity by adding a service provider in Windows Parental Controls, such as Microsoft®'s Windows Live Family Safety. The Family Safety web filter needs to be installed and set up on each computer your children use. You can download and install Windows Live Family Safety for free from explore.live.com/windows-live-family-safety.

Basic precautions
The most sensible advice for parents is to spend time with their children when they are using the internet. Putting the PC the children use for web surfing in a communal part of the house, like the hall or lounge, makes it more difficult for them to access undesirable content without your knowledge. You also have plenty of opportunities to discuss the internet and how they plan to use it. You can even help with their homework! Make sure you know what they are doing, that they can talk to you about it and you can help them understand the risks. Also let them see you are there to help them if they have a question or problem. Don't let them fear your anger or they won't confide if they have a problem. You can also limit the time they spend on the internet: a child spending excessive periods on the internet or being evasive about what they are doing should be a worrying sign. Make sure it doesn't interfere with their real life.

In general, informing a child is usually a lot easier than trying to outsmart them. The advice you can give them includes following the SMART rule for children (from the Internet Watch Foundation, www.iwf.org.uk). It is worth taking the time to go through these rules with your children and check they understand them and agree to abide by them. In essence the dangers are very similar to those that children are warned about outside the internet and the actions to be taken are just common sense:

- **S** – Keep your personal details **Secret**. Never use a parent's credit card without their permission, and never give away your name, address or passwords: it's like giving away the keys to your home.

- **M** – Never **Meet** someone you have contacted in cyberspace without your parents'/carers' permission, and only when they can be present.

- **A** – Don't **Accept** emails, open attachments or download files from people or organisations you don't really know or trust. They may contain viruses or nasty messages.

- **R** – **Remember** that someone you meet online may not be who they say they are. If you feel worried or uncomfortable in a chat room simply get out of there.

- **T** – **Tell** your parent or carer if someone or something in cyberspace makes you feel uncomfortable or worried.

Children often spend a lot of time on social networking websites like Facebook®. Further details on Facebook® security are given later in this chapter, but for children it is worth giving them some specific advice:

- They should not be sharing their location or address on websites because it could expose them to contact from strangers and provides unnecessary personal details.

- They should avoid filling out questionnaires, free giveaways online contests etc. because these are typically used to obtain personal information for marketing reasons.

- They should look for and check the opt-out buttons on websites wherever possible to prevent their personal information from being collected and used.

Finally children have a right to privacy. Some might feel they cannot share a problem with their parents (e.g. if they have relationship or parental problem). In these cases, the child can seek the help of charities. The National Society for the Prevention of Cruelty to Children (NSPCC at www.nspcc.org) has advice on how to delete temporary folders and history files to ensure genuine pleas for help do not get found out by abusers. Most teenagers would resent their phone conversations being 'bugged', so they should have some expectation of keeping their online communications private too.

Some useful websites
There are many good websites to get further help and advice on children's use of the internet:

www.iwf.org.uk	The website for the Internet Watch Foundation, an industry funded body with a hotline to report illegal material. It also has more information (and links to reviews) about filtering software.

www.childnet-int.org	The website for Childnet International, a not-for-profit organisation aiming to make the internet a safe place for children.
www.safekids.com	Online safety advice.
www.kidsmart.org.uk	Helping children to be smart with their internet use.
www.thinkuknow.co.uk	Child Exploitation and Online Protection Centre, with help and information effectively targeted at different age groups.
www.cybermentors.org.uk	Helping to beat cyberbullying.
www.anti-bullyingalliance.org.uk	
www.chatdanger.com	Specific safety advice for chat rooms provided by Childnet.
www.childline.org.uk	The website for the children's charity ChildLine with a free 24-hour helpline number for children and young people in danger – 0800 1111.

Cyber bullying and harassment

It is sometimes difficult as adults to appreciate the pain and anguish that cyber bullying can cause to young people. The old adage of 'sticks and stones may break my bones but names can never hurt me' is not at all helpful. There have been instances where someone has been driven to suicide by cyber bullying. Young people today are so embedded with their online and mobile communications that hurtful comments are much more vivid to them than to those of us that weren't brought up with the ever-present internet, or manage to keep semi-detached from the increasingly virtual modern lifestyle. To make matters worse, the bullying of old was restricted to school time or time spent in the company of the abusers. Now it can be 24/7, a violation of someone's privacy and hope of respite. The effects of cyber bullying and harassment must not be underplayed.

If you are a victim of stalking, harassment or bullying, then seriously consider going to the police. Under the UK's Protection from Harassment Act 1997, you may only need two occurrences before the police can act. Try to gather evidence for them such as:

- Make a copy of any relevant emails or chat room conversations. If you hold down the 'Alt' key and press 'Prt Sc – SysRq' or 'PrintScreen' on a Windows® PC keyboard, the computer will take a copy of what is on your screen. Open up a new document and paste the image into it. If not shown on original, then add the time and date of the conversation and the day's date.

- If you are being harassed on social networking websites such as Facebook®, Bebo®, Myspace® etc. you should block the perpetrator immediately.

- Social networking sites should also have a 'panic button'. This allows youngsters to immediately report suspicious behaviour to the UK police Child Exploitation and Online Protection Centre (CEOP).

- Change your social network privacy settings so only friends can see your information.

- If the cyber bully has set up an imposter profile, then you should report it to the social networking website. You should also ask everyone you know on your 'friends list' to post a message exposing the impostor and that they should block that profile.

- If they are making rude comments, then you can also report those individually.

- If you are being harassed via email, then you can block it in Outlook® by clicking **Message→Block Sender…**, but don't do this if you want to keep the emails as potential evidence.

Content filtering

As we all know, the internet contains a good deal of potentially offensive content and we do not want children stumbling across it. We can ensure that they cannot access inappropriate websites by performing content filtering.

The simplest way to do this is to use the mechanism known as Content Advisor in the Internet Explorer® browser. This allows you to specify what types of internet content your browser can access. Content is broken down into four categories: language, nudity, sex and violence, and each can be rated on a scale of 0–4 using the RSACi content rating system* (Table 4.1). Websites rate themselves on the four categories using this scale. Content Advisor allows you to set the ratings you want to be filtered out so that websites above those ratings are blocked.

The main drawback with the RSACi system is that it is voluntary. It is up to the website owners to rate their website. Although many websites have rated

Table 4.1 RSACi Rating System

Level	Language	Nudity	Sex	Violence
0	Inoffensive slang	None	None	None
1	Mild expletives	Revealing attire	Passionate kissing	Fighting
2	Moderate expletives	Partial nudity	Clothed sexual touching	Killing
3	Obscene gestures	Frontal nudity	Non-explicit sexual touching	Killing with blood and gore
4	Explicit or crude language	Provocative frontal nudity	Explicit sexual activity	Gratuitous and wanton violence

*RSACi – Recreational Software Advisory Council on the Internet (RSACi)

themselves many have not and your browser may block them even though they are perfectly OK to view. On the other hand, some malicious websites may have rated themselves too low and may still be accessible but offensive. To overcome the first problem Content Advisor allows you to set a supervisor password so that unrated websites, which have been blocked, can still be viewed on a case-by-case basis. Naturally parents should keep this password to themselves!

Be aware that Content Advisor can be bypassed and children may find a way round it, perhaps by downloading another browser with the settings applied differently. If you feel you need a stronger mechanism to control content you may need to look at some of the commercial tools available (some of the following have free trials for download), for example Netnanny, Cyberpatrol, Cybersitter, Norton Parental Control, Windows Live Family Safety etc.

Using Content Advisor

You can enable Content Advisor by selecting **Tools→Internet Options** and clicking the **Content** tab. If you choose to enable the feature, you will be prompted for the supervisor password that allows you to change the settings and override the filter if necessary. You can then select each of the four content categories and choose which settings you wish to filter by moving the slider control between 0 and 4. Click **OK** when you have finished making the selections, but do not forget your password! Now, if you attempt to browse a website with an RSACi rating higher than any of your settings you will get a dialogue box telling you that it has been blocked. The dialogue box also allows you to type in the supervisor password to override the block.

Unrated websites will also initially be blocked and can be unblocked with the password. If you find many of your favourite websites unrated and typing in the password is irritating, then you will either have to change your password to something short and quick to type (though obviously this will be insecure) or allow unrated websites to be viewed (with the obvious risk that harmful content could now be seen).

You can change the supervisor password by selecting **Tools→Internet Options** and click the **Content** tab. Under **Content Advisor**, click **Settings**, type in your password and click **OK**. Then select the **General** tab and you will see a dialogue with a button labelled **Change Password**.

To allow unrated sites to be viewed without requiring the supervisor password, select **Tools→Internet Options** and click the **Content** tab. Under **Content Advisor**, click **Settings** and type in your password and click **OK**. Then select the **General** tab and you will see a dialogue box (as above for changing password) with two tick boxes. You can select **Users can see sites that have no rating**.

You can also select websites that are always approved or always blocked regardless of their rating. Go to **Tools→Internet Options** and click the **Content** tab. Under **Content Advisor**, click **Settings** and type in your password and click **OK**. Then select the **Approved Sites** tab and you will see a dialogue box that allows you to type in a web address and then click either **Always** to permit it or **Never** to forbid it.

An alternative approach for younger children is to set up a 'safe' home page for Internet Explorer® using **Tools→Internet Options**. Type in the preferred address. Some examples of children-only websites (particularly for younger children) are www.safekids.com and www.yahooligans.com.

You are probably aware that web searches often turn up links to dubious looking websites and this is clearly a risk for children as they start to browse the web more widely. Some websites have special search engines that are pre-filtered for safe searches. At www.google.com, for example, there is a 'SafeSearch' facility designed to keep sexually explicit content out of search results.

Computer game consoles

Many computer game consoles nowadays can make use of an internet connection for multi-player games. Some also have the ability to provide web browsing and thus the risks discussed above from children accessing inappropriate material arise and need to be addressed. One of the key risks from game consoles arises because they are often in bedrooms or not accessed frequently by parents as PCs often are. Some parents may not be aware that unrestricted web browsing is available. The Sony PS3, for example, has a built-in web browser and a large hard drive that can store many images and films.

On the PS3, you can set a parental control on the web browser and use a web filter to block inappropriate websites. Look in the **Internet Browser Start Control** under **Settings** and **Security Settings** to restrict the ability to start the browser.

Note that this still provides access to the PS3 network for gaming (that's the point of the internet access after all), but this gaming may include chatting with strangers. In this case, the discussion in the next section of how to make children aware of the risks from internet chat is even more important.

Chat rooms

Another problem comes from email or chat room conversations. Chat rooms are places on the internet that allow people to meet and exchange messages. The messages are typed and become visible to everyone in the chat room almost instantaneously. Chat rooms are very popular, especially with young children and teenagers. The problem is that there is no guarantee that the other people in the chat room are children. It is not possible to confirm who they are. This makes chat rooms a venue for paedophiles or potential abusers to make contact with children. They may try and build a relationship over several months and try to arrange a meeting with them, or gradually use suggestive language to attempt to 'groom' a child for sexual contact. Unfortunately for children, surfing the internet from the safety of home may give them a false sense of security. They may start to see the person they are chatting with as a friend, but that person may not even be another child!

Chat room conversations are generally open and visible to all members of the chat room, but it is also possible to have private one-to-one chats and this is where the main danger can arise. Advise your children to stay in the public areas of chat rooms. Children need to realise that all contacts in chat rooms are strangers and they must never give out personal details, especially their full name, address or phone number.

If something unpleasant happens to someone in a chat room they should immediately leave. Some chat rooms have so-called panic buttons and some have ways of blocking messages from anyone who is bothering them.

Some chat rooms are moderated. This means the messages are checked periodically for the nature of the conversations and to try and ensure personal details are not divulged. These, and any other chat rooms that seem safe, can be marked as 'favourites' or 'bookmarks' in your internet browser. Your children should agree that these are the only ones they should use. Remind them that you can check on their web browsing, but you don't really want to.

If you think your child may be being contacted by a paedophile or has been sent inappropriate or illegal material, then you should certainly contact the police.

Copyright theft
Copyright theft is a widely practised abuse that costs various industries and artists many billions of pounds. From the copying of games in the playground, to copying and distributing music on the internet, to illicit recordings of movies yet to be released on video or DVD, the breach of copyright is costing the artists involved their legitimate licence fees for their work. Companies are losing money that could be put into more works or cheaper prices. Copyright theft hurts all honest consumers paying the retail price.

Children and hackers
So far in this section we have talked about protecting children from internet abuse, but many children go on to become a cause of concern for computer security. They become computer hackers. What can we do to discourage this?

We need to realise that computer hackers are not necessarily the clever nerds or geeks they are usually portrayed as. Many hacking attacks are codified in small software applications that anyone can run as an automated hacking tool. This has led to the term 'script-kiddies' for hackers who use automated tools without understanding exactly what they do or how they do it (unlike the cognoscenti hackers who designed and built the tools knowing they would be inviting many others to use them). Any child with a healthy interest in computers and the internet could potentially become a criminal hacker and cause businesses and individuals a lot of trouble. They could also make a lot of trouble for themselves and their families because such acts can lead to imprisonment.

There are various types of hacking that children commonly get mixed up in and we, as parents and responsible IT users, need to be able to tell our children that they are wrong, why they are wrong and what could happen if they become criminal hackers.

A lot of hackers get a thrill from breaking and entering into computer systems. They might guess passwords or run special scripts to break in, but just doing this, without any malicious intent and without disturbing the contents of the computer itself, is harmful and illegal. Many people seek to defend this type of hacking along the lines of 'we didn't change anything', 'we only looked around' and 'no one came to any harm'. Unfortunately 'just looking' can do a lot of harm because if the computer managers have detected the intrusion they have to make certain nothing was changed. Without a full and thorough investigation, which is time-consuming and costly, they have no way of knowing whether they can still trust that computer system. There is always the possibility of such a break-in leading to an accidental disruption of the system, which could be even more expensive particularly in a business critical system.

If the intrusion is taken one step further there are yet more consequences depending on what data has been changed or deleted. Children can get pleasure by changing exam results in school computers for example, but this is fraud. It may just seem like a funny prank, but it wouldn't seem so funny if someone was doing it to their results.

If a young person is caught hacking it is considered a serious offence and the authorities will investigate thoroughly. They may well prosecute, and some young hackers have gone to prison. Even without prison, a criminal record can make it difficult to get a job or go to university. Computer companies are wary of employing anyone with a hacking background for fear of damaging their reputation and credibility. Someone with an interest in computers, who hacks, could find themselves cut off from the very activity he or she loves.

Children must recognise the consequences of hacking so they can make a mature and responsible decision not to get involved. Hacking is illegal, causes serious and expensive problems for the victims, and people go to jail for it.

PROTECTING YOUR PRIVACY

Privacy is your right to keep information about you confidential. It is a fundamental human right, recognised by the United Nations in its Universal Declaration of Human Rights in 1948. So what has privacy to do with computers and information?

Your right to be left alone can only be protected through confidentiality of the information about you. Let's take some examples. A fundamental piece of information about you is whether you exist or not. If you have a birth certificate, you are in a record somewhere, held by the government, as being alive. This piece of information, that you exist, is not something that any person usually worries whether it is secret or not. If you wanted to be a hermit and to completely separate yourself from society, then you might want this to be the only piece of information about you. If there were further information, perhaps with your address – 1 Lonely Cave, Distant Mountain, Forgotten Country, Nowhere-on-Earth – then you could now be tracked down and your right to be left alone could be violated. You might want your address to be known by some friends or relatives, but not by people you wanted to avoid (the rest of society in the hypothetical hermit case). So privacy is about your control over the information that exists about you. Is it accurate? Who knows it? What can they do with it? Who can they tell it to? You privacy is invaded if this information is disclosed or forged when it shouldn't be. You want to preserve your control over the properties of this information. It is an information security problem.

This is especially true nowadays when so much information about us is stored on computers, but what harm can it do us if our privacy is violated? Perhaps the people most concerned with privacy to date are the wealthy and the famous. This is because they tend to be of interest to many people and their private lives are often discussed and analysed by the media. What they do in public view is information that is a public 'fact'. What they do in private is private. But where are the boundaries? I do my shopping in public, but does this give my credit card company the right to make my credit card bills public? Such an occurrence was embarrassing to a British politician some years ago. In the USA, a senior judge's records of videos he rented were published just as he was being considered for the Supreme Court – he did not make it perhaps due in part to the type of videos he had been found to rent.

Wherever information is gathered about us we need to be concerned that it is safeguarded by those that have it. This is usually known as 'data protection'. It means that our privacy must be protected by the setting of rules, policies and limits on the collection, handling and use of personal information gathered by companies doing their business over the internet. E-commerce raises new concerns about privacy because much more information about individuals can be collected, and if privacy is not safeguarded there is the potential for a much more widespread and serious impact to the data subject – you.

What information might be a privacy problem in cyberspace? Firstly, new information could be created about you by watching your surfing habits. What sorts of websites do you visit? What sort of things do you purchase? Then there is information you may have given out in return for access to a website: your career and job title, address etc. This information can sometimes be amalgamated to provide a detailed picture of you to target you with advertising for specific products.

Websites have four main ways to collect information about you:

- Basic information provided by the browser.
- Forms you submit.
- Tracking your use, for example with spyware.
- Cookies – small data files left on your PC by a website for later use.

Browser information
As you browse the web, your web browser keeps track of information about your activities. It keeps a track of the websites you visit in a 'History' list. It may keep a copy of the websites on your hard drive as a temporary file so that if you go back to that website and it is unchanged it can load the page from the disk rather than downloading it again. The addresses of websites you have visited are used by some browsers to provide an 'auto-complete' service. This is when you start to type a website name into the 'Address' box at the top of the browser and a suggested address is completed for you. This can save the time of typing a long address. Auto-complete can also work for data you have typed in forms and for usernames and passwords to websites. None of this information is actually sent by the browser to websites, although there is sometimes concern that vulnerabilities exist that can allow an unscrupulous website to get it, or a malicious piece of software could access it.

This sort of information is certainly visible to other users of your PC. If you wish to control this browser information to protect your privacy, then in Internet Explorer® 7:

To control Auto-complete, click **Tools→Internet Options→Content**, and by AutoComplete click **Settings**. This gives you the option to restrict AutoComplete for any or all of: forms, web addresses, and usernames and passwords.

In **Tools→Internet Options→General**, under Browsing history, click **Delete...** to get options to delete:

- temporary internet files;
- cookies (but note that deleting these may cause you some problems with some shopping websites, see below);
- browsing history;
- form data (to delete data you have previously typed into forms and is accessible to AutoComplete;
- passwords (you should only save non-sensitive passwords, all others should be deleted).

Note that your browsing history starts to build up again after you have cleared out the history record. You can reduce the number of websites stored in your history list by selecting a small number for the 'Days to keep pages in history'. Similarly, temporary files will start to build up as you browse, and these will need regular clearing. In fact your browser potentially tells the world a great deal of information, which can include:

- the website you viewed prior to the current page;
- the website you click on from the current page;
- the type of browser you are using;
- your computer's operating system details;
- your computer's IP address;
- any files or images downloaded on the page.

You can check to see what information your browser is keeping by going to www.privacy.net and clicking on the privacy analysis service you can find on the website.

Internet Explorer® versions 8 and 9 have additional privacy features known as InPrivate Browsing and InPrivate Filtering. InPrivate Browsing prevents the browser from storing details of your browsing on your PC so that it cannot be seen by other users you share the computer with. You can turn it on by clicking on **Safety→InPrivate Browsing**. A new window will open up and InPrivate Browsing is active only whilst you browse in this window. Another way to start it is by opening a tab and clicking on the **Browse with InPrivate** link. You finish using InPrivate when you close the InPrivate window. Note that there is an indicator by the address bar that displays 'InPrivate' in bold as a reminder when you are using it.

InPrivate filtering allows you to protect your privacy from websites that track your activities. Some websites, such as some advertisers', may track the web pages you browse so they can collect information about your interests. This helps them to aim advertisements at you. InPrivate Filtering will analyse websites, and if it finds one embedded with this type of tracking code, it will give you the option to block it. It can also give you the option to block these embedded or 'third-party' websites automatically. In Internet Explorer® versions 8 and 9 go to **Safety→InPrivate Filtering** and select the option to block automatically these websites or to block them manually. In the latter case you can click **Choose content to block** or allow and specify any websites you either do or do not trust.

Note that everything you do on the web and every piece of information you see or send goes through your Internet Service Provider (ISP). If you do not trust your ISP (at least check their privacy policy) or a government with access to your ISP records, then you will need a much more extreme approach to surfing the web using something called 'encrypted tunnelling'. Anonymizer.com (www.anonymizer.com) provides web address encryption to hide surfing habits from an ISP. It also provides other services, such as the removal of cookies, Java® and JavaScript®, anonymous surfing and anonymous email.

Submitting forms

Most reputable websites publish a privacy policy in order to comply with data protection legislation or to show their recognition of the principles of data protection. The policy can usually be accessed from a link on the home page (sometimes on every page) of a website. Although the advice is to read these policies, in practice they are rather long and only parts are relevant. If you are giving out significant personal information, then try to read the policy. It is also a good precaution to read it if you are unsure of the reputation of the organisation collecting the data.

Website forms require many information boxes to be filled in. Quite often the mandatory ones are marked with an asterisk. Don't bother to fill in boxes that are not marked because there is no need to give away more information than you need to. Check to see if the website gives you the option to tell it not to retain your information for later use or to prevent it from providing the information to third parties. Some websites or forms allow you to tick a box to prevent an organisation from passing your data on to a third party or contacting you. Look carefully for such boxes and select your preferred options.

Spyware

Spyware is software that surreptitiously keeps a track of things you do on your computer, such as the websites you visit, or obtains personal data about you from your PC. It can arrive on your PC in a number of ways. It can be downloaded unobtrusively from an untrustworthy website, especially if the security settings on your internet browser are set too low. It can arrive as part of a piece of software that you have downloaded on purpose from the web – often this could be in file-sharing and music-sharing applications. Spyware can be present in some freeware and shareware, as well as in media players. A good personal firewall should alert you to some outbound attempts by Trojans, but spyware may attempt to send the information it has gathered back to the spy master by more subtle means, perhaps as part of a normal web browsing session. Adware is another type of spyware. Adware is software designed to track your surfing habits in order to show you relevant advertisements via weblinks. More detail on this is given in Chapter 6.

You will need specialist software to detect and eliminate spyware and adware. There are two particularly renowned pieces of software that can find and allow you to delete adware and spyware: they are called 'Ad-Aware' (www.lavasoft.com) and 'Spybot – Search and Destroy®' (www.safer-networking.org). Both are very similar to anti-virus software in that they recognise a long list of programs known to be adware or spyware. At the time of writing, the tools are free for personal use. As well as finding and removing spyware and adware, they can also detect keyloggers and diallers, clean up your surfing tracks, and have an update function to ensure you are protected against the latest threats.

Security software is a fast changing business. The threats change and the attack methods become ever more ingenious, so it's difficult to give any precise recommendations on software to use. A little research can save you money and get you good software. Not all free software is necessarily the best, but there is usually a free product that sets the benchmark for commercial products to beat. The website www.download.com has a wide variety of software for free download: either free products or free trials. It also has reviews and shows how many times software has been downloaded. In one week alone Ad-Aware was downloaded over 2 million times!

Cookies

A cookie is a small piece of data that a website uses to store information about you on your hard disk. Whenever you visit that website it retrieves the cookie it previously saved and the website uses it to 'remember' your preferences or account information. By recalling this information about you it can then customise the website. E-commerce websites use cookies to identify you and to record relevant customer information, such as your preferences and delivery address. They can save you retyping this information every time you visit the website. Cookies can also store your buying habits. This allows the website to tailor offers and promotions potentially of interest to you.

Cookies are designed to improve the web surfing experience and they are used by most commercial websites. They are very small files, they cannot carry viruses and they only contain information about you that you have agreed to give to the website (or information taken from your browser). The main security feature is that a website should only be able to view the cookies that it stored. It should not be able to see cookies set up by other websites.

From a privacy point of view, the only risk from cookies should be that if someone else gets access to your PC they can see information about your web surfing habits and they may be able to assume your identity in certain transactions (if not protected by a password). However, the mechanism that prevents websites seeing cookies from other websites has been circumvented. Web advertisers embed their adverts in many different companies' web pages. They can therefore store a cookie each time they show you an advert and track the websites you surf. They can integrate the information from lots of cookies to get a detailed profile of you from your web surfing, the adverts you click on and the things you buy.

It is possible to disable cookies in your browser (as mentioned above). If you do this you will find that some websites, usually commercial websites, will give you an error message. Some may not work properly and some may not even work at all. If you want to take care with cookies you could disable them and see how it affects your favourite websites, but it is likely to be rather inconvenient. If you set up your browser to prompt you whenever a website uses cookies, then you will probably find yourself irritated by the number of times you are asked whether you wish to accept a cookie. If you enable cookies, then you are exposed to the risks that cookies bring. If you find disabling or prompting for cookies irritating, then there are some free tools you can download to help manage your cookies.

To manage cookies in Internet Explorer® versions 7, 8 and 9: Click **Tools→Internet Options→Privacy**. You will see a slider with six separate settings for cookies, ranging from 'Accept All' as the lowest setting, to 'Block All' as the highest setting.

Start with a high setting and see how often you get warning messages. If they become too irritating, gradually lower the threshold to the highest you can tolerate.

You can also set up a customised policy from the **Privacy** tab by clicking the **Advanced** button. This gives you three options (Allow, Prompt or Block) for first-party cookies and third-party cookies. First-party cookies come from the website you are currently viewing. They are often used by e-commerce websites to remember you and your preferences from one visit to the next. Many websites may not work properly without them and in general they are worth allowing. Third-party cookies, on the other hand, come from websites other than the one you are viewing, such as links to advertisers on the web page. If you allow these, then your surfing information may be picked up by websites that are unknown to you. I would advise blocking third-party cookies. This is unlikely to detract from your web browsing experience.

SOCIABLE NETWORKING

The key issue with social networking is to protect your privacy, as discussed in the preceding section. Most social networking websites, such as Facebook®, Myspace®, LinkedIn® etc. have options for you to control whether the information you enter can be seen by other web users. The way they do this can be different in each case, but we will take Facebook® as an example and describe some of the privacy options you can use. If you use other social networking websites, just explore their option settings to take control of your privacy. Before we do this for Facebook®, it is worth noting that anything put on these websites has the potential to be copied and distributed around the web and to last forever. If pictures or comments are posted that could embarrass you or lead a potential employer to think you are unreliable, then your posts may come back to haunt you. The best advice here is not to post anything that could give anyone a negative impression of you, even if your friends think it funny and happily post embarrassing material. Just don't do it. Employers are increasingly using social websites to get some feedback about possible recruits, and friends and relations may find out things about you that you would wish to keep private. You have been warned!

You should also take the sorts of precautions that, by reading this book, you are now well aware of. Don't just click on links or download software if you have any doubts about where they came from. In short:

- be careful what you post or communicate;
- be sceptical;
- be alert for scams and possible malware;
- control your privacy.

Privacy controls generally cover four areas:

- Who can see the things you share?
- Who can see your personal data?
- Can your data be found by search engines like Google®?
- What data is accessible by apps that you use?

In Facebook®, at time of writing, the default for who can see the things you share is 'Everyone'. To change this, go to your **Profile** page and click **Privacy settings**, then click **Profile Information** and scroll down to **Posts by Me** where you can select **Only Friends**. Similarly in **Profile Information** check your **Personal Info** settings and other information such as **Birthday**. Again restricting this to 'Only Friends' is sensible. Finally, the best way to restrict your exposure to search engines is to go to the **Search settings** page and see if the word 'Allow' is ticked. If so, then search engines can access and index any information you've marked as visible by 'Everyone'. To prevent this, in **Privacy Settings**, click **Search** and untick the box labelled **Allow**. You may wonder why this is worth doing bearing in mind that such information is already visible by everyone, but it is a useful precaution to take against fraudsters or identity thieves who may be looking to identify victims. To control apps, go to **Account**, choose **Privacy Settings**, then click **Edit your settings** under 'Applications and Websites' at the bottom. Then, next to 'Applications you use', choose **Edit Settings**. Here, you can see which applications you've author-ised to interact with your account and when you authorised them. You can also see what permissions the apps have by clicking **Edit Settings**. Some will allow this to be controlled or, if you don't like their level of access, you can delete them.

It is worth noting that social networking websites can and do change their privacy policies and settings. It is in their interests for their members to share as much as possible because it provides them with free material, more links and page views and ultimately more advertising revenue. It may seem cool to have a large number of online friends, but it is a security risk.

Another feature of Facebook® worth remembering is 'Remote logoff'. If you use a computer whilst travelling, or at a friend's house or library say, and forget to log off, then you can do so remotely thereby preventing someone from getting access to your account. In **Account Settings and Account Security** there is a section that tells you from which computers you have used Facebook® and whether you are still logged in. Clicking **End Activity** will close that session down. The Account Security box also allows you to set up warnings by text or email if a new PC or mobile logs in to your account. It is also possible to 'untag' yourself from a Facebook® photo to protect your privacy further.

Finally, don't announce on Facebook® when you are going on holiday or when you are out of the house, it is just an invitation to burglars – it may seem obvious, but many people have done it. Also you are best advised not to use Facebook® for party invitations (in fact keep your address well out of it) because some people have found the invitation spreads and suddenly hundreds of undesirable party-goers are descending on your little soirée. Teenagers especially should be made aware of this risk!

ERASING DATA ON YOUR PC

As you can see from the example of cookies and the web browser, your software leaves a lot of information on your computer's hard drive in files that you might not normally look at or know about. These are files such as temporary files, system files, back-up files etc. and they may contain information that you did not realise was actually present on your hard disk.

If you want to sell or pass on your PC to another user you clearly need to delete this information and any other personal information, files or sensitive records. You might think the simplest way to do this is just to delete the files. Unfortunately this does not securely delete the data. Anyone with the correct software can find what was on the PC. When you delete a file (or format a drive) the operating system simply removes the 'index' to the file from the folder. In effect it forgets the file exists and stops protecting it from being overwritten on the disk. The bits (the 1s and 0s) that make up the file are not changed – the data in the file still exists and will continue to exist (even if the operating system tells you the file itself doesn't) until new 1s and 0s from a new file are put on the disk in the space previously occupied by the deleted file.

If you just delete files from your hard drive prior to selling it, then it is easy for someone with the correct tool to recreate the files and any personal information therein. You need special tools that will deliberately overwrite the disk in such a way that the previous information is completely obliterated.

SUMMARY

- Your web browser can be configured to reduce many of the privacy and security risks of surfing the net.

- Be suspicious of anything unusual when shopping or banking on the web. Be aware of potential frauds and scams.

- Make use of the 'zones' feature to ensure that you are adequately protected against malicious web content from websites that are new to you.

- Take the following precautions when undertaking financial transactions over the web:

  - Always check the website address is what you expect it to be. Never click links in email messages.

  - Make sure the website uses SSL. Check for the padlock symbol and the 'https' prefix in the address. Verify the certificate.

  - Use a credit card, never a debit card. Allocate one with a low credit limit specifically for web transactions.

- Talk to your children about the risks of using the web. Make sure they know never to give out personal information and never to arrange to meet anyone they have contacted over the internet.

- Put the children's internet PC in a part of the house where it can be seen whilst they are on it.

- Set up content filtering and parental control in your browser if your children use it.

- Make sure older children understand why hacking is wrong.

- Report cyberstalkers and any harassment on the internet to the appropriate authorities.

- Try not to give out too much personal information. Read privacy policies.

- Always use a special purpose disk cleaner tool to wipe personal data securely if you are disposing of an old PC.

5 EMAIL SECURITY

Email was one of the earliest internet applications and is one of the most used. In essence, it is the ability to send messages between two computers: a source and a destination. The messages travel with no guarantee that delivery will happen within any given time, or indeed happen at all. It is like the conventional post except there is only third-class email! The other difference is that every email is, in fact, the electronic equivalent of a postcard. The contents of the email are open and plainly visible to anyone (or any computer) handling it, as it travels from source to destination. The way the internet works is that an email, or any communication, can pass through many intermediaries en route.

To see this, try the following in Microsoft® Outlook Express®. Click to select the email you wish to examine. Click the **File** command and select **Properties**, then click the **Details** tab. You will see a screen of text known as the header of the email message. This stores information like the time and date the message was received and sent, and also tracks the IP addresses and URLs (see Chapter 2) of the computers that have acted as the links between source and destination. They usually appear in and after a line that starts 'Received:'.

Interception of email is not a significant threat unless you intend to send a valuable piece of information like your credit card number. Do not send valuable information by email just in case someone is snooping or gets access to your mailbox or the mail at your email service provider. Remember that emails could be forwarded anywhere, by accident or mistake, or the computer or computers it goes to may be compromised by a virus. It is unlikely, but possible. As we saw in Chapter 4 there are secure ways to send credit card information to websites. If you really want to keep your emails confidential, then you will need to use encryption, which we will discuss later in this chapter. Let's look at the general measures you can take against a range of email threats.

BASIC PRECAUTIONS

The main risk from the widespread use of email is the high likelihood of receiving a virus. We will learn more about viruses in Chapter 6, but before we consider what they do and how they do it we first need to look at some measures to protect ourselves from those borne by email.

The main objective of a virus (indeed of any hacker attempt to infiltrate your system) is to be able to run a program on your machine. Once you have let a malicious program run, then you are in trouble. The program can even hide itself so you may have no idea you are infected. Having an up-to-date anti-virus tool is critical, as well as browsing the web from a Standard user account, as discussed previously.

Emails received and displayed in HTML format (the same as a web page) can contain malicious scripts just like some web pages. Internet zone security is important here: Outlook®, uses the same security constraints as you have set up in Internet Explorer®.

Many viruses propagate as attachments to emails. It follows that whenever you double-click on an attachment you are taking a great risk. If you receive an unexpected attachment by email, the safest thing to do is delete it and ask the sender to send it again after making sure that it is virus-free and not the result of the propagation of a worm. It can't hurt to resend it, so it's better safe than sorry.

If an attachment is a .exe, .vbs or .doc (.docx) file, then it is particularly dangerous. A .exe file contains an executable program, a .vbs file contains a Visual Basic® program and a .doc (.docx) file contains a word-processing file. You might think that this latter file should be safe, but Word, along with Excel® (.xls, .xlsx) and Access (.mdb, .accdb), it has the capability to execute small programs known as macros. These programs are used to perform automation within a word-processing document, but a virus writer can embed a malicious macro inside a Word document that runs as soon as the document is opened. So even .doc files and .xls files can be dangerous.

Some virus writers have exploited bugs in Outlook® to disguise the type of file in the attachment. Some older versions of Outlook® do not check the type of file, so a file with a seemingly innocuous extension could, in reality, be one of the dangerous types. Another bug fails to recognise an attachment with a double extension, for example .txt.doc. The affected versions of Outlook® only display .txt and the user may think it is safe to double-click. These bugs have been fixed in recent releases, but they are indicative of the type of problem to look out for.

The virus that reached you by email will also look to continue its journey and infect more people. When you double-click the attachment, the virus has an opportunity to run a malicious payload on your PC and also to spread itself by email. Some will email themselves to email addresses in your Outlook® address book. You have then helped to pass on the infection to your friends.

Configuring Outlook®
Just as with the web browser, your email software can carry personal information in the form of a profile. You can modify the profile so you do not give away any private information:

In Outlook Express®, select **Tools→Accounts...→Mail**. Select the email account you want to modify and then click **Properties**. In the Properties dialogue box, click the **General** tab and in User Information remove any personal information (perhaps replace your name with 'Anonymous'). Similarly in Outlook® 2007 (or later) you can look in **Tools→Account Settings** and then click the account you wish to configure. Click **Change** to check what personal information is associated with the account.

Accidental security compromise can occur by sending emails to the wrong person. Notice that in Outlook® and Outlook Express® the icons for 'Reply', 'Reply All' and 'Forward' are next to each other on the toolbar. You can forward a comment on an email you received to someone you trust, only to find that you have accidentally sent it to everyone who received the first email – not just your friend – by hitting the 'Reply All' button by mistake. A simple tip to avoid this is to customise your toolbar. Either remove the icon for 'Reply All' or move it well away from the 'Forward' and 'Reply' buttons.

Some years ago Microsoft® introduced a preview pane into Outlook® and Outlook Express®. This enabled a selected email to be partially displayed (previewed) from within the window. Double-clicking on the email launched it in a new window as per normal. Very few people would have thought that this preview capability could be a security risk. In order to preview the email, the software is in fact opening the email in a very similar way as you would do by double-clicking it. An attacker who embedded malicious commands in an email could force those commands to be run when the email was opened and would not need human intervention at all. The mere previewing of the email would run the commands. So even if you suspected the email to come from a dubious source and wanted to delete it, it might be too late once Outlook®/Outlook Express® had previewed it. This problem was fixed, but is indicative of what can happen if a system is not kept secure and up to date.

SECURE EMAIL USING ENCRYPTION

We have mentioned encryption several times in the course of this book and now is the time to understand how it works and what it offers us in the way of secure communication. It can offer confidentiality. We can make a message unreadable to anyone apart from the intended recipient by encrypting (or scrambling) it. We will see how to achieve this shortly. Encryption can also provide integrity: its digital signature can be used to show whether a message has been changed in transit. A digital signature can also show authenticity of the message by proving who sent it.

A very useful approach to encryption is known as Public Key Cryptography (PKC). This type of encryption works by using pairs of keys to lock or unlock files just as physical keys can lock or unlock doors. Of each pair, one is made public and one is kept private, very private. If the public key is used to scramble a message, then only the private key can unscramble it and vice versa. To send a confidential message to someone I need to use **their** public key to scramble the message. I know that if they have kept their private key private, then they will be the only person able to unscramble the email. However, this doesn't ensure the message has not been changed, after all anyone could use the public key to send the message. To prove that the message is unchanged I also use **my** private key to scramble it. The recipient unscrambles it with my public key. The recipient now knows for sure that it came from me because my public key unscrambled it successfully. A different key would not. If the two messages are the same, then the recipient also knows that the message has not been changed.

The process of using a private key to scramble a message is known as signing. Private keys are stored on your PC and must be kept confidential. Public keys are usually contained, along with details, such as the name of the owner, dates of validity etc., in a digital certificate sometimes known as a digital ID.

Public Key Cryptography is the basis for most encryption systems. There are three different systems in fairly common use on the internet and you will need to choose which one you want to use. The deciding factor will probably be the types of systems being used by the people you want to communicate with because it is not possible to send encrypted email between the different systems.

Secure MIME*

MIME is the default secure message format for Outlook® and Outlook Express®. It allows secure messages to be exchanged with users of other email software as long as they are also Secure MIME compatible.

The first step to secure email is to obtain a digital certificate. In Outlook Express®, select **Tools→Options**... and click the **Security** tab. Under **Secure Mail**, click **Get Digital ID...** and you will be taken to a website where you can choose a Certificate Authority (CA), a company that issues certificates. (In Outlook 2007 or later, go to **Tools→Trust Center...→E-mail Security**.) The CA website will contain instructions on how to register and purchase a digital ID. Once obtained, you need to take good care of the private key mentioned above (your browser should assign a password to protect it and you should choose a strong one). You should also make a back-up of the private key and the digital ID and store them in a safe place (such as a safe). Backing up, and restoring, can be achieved using the Import/Export Digital ID dialogue box available by selecting **Tools→Options...→Security**. Click the **Digital IDs** button and then the **Import...** or **Export...** button as required. Follow the instructions given to you by the Wizard that appears.

Now you can use the certificates. To sign a message in Outlook Express®, compose it as usual but before clicking on Send, select **Tools→Digitally Sign** and a red ribbon will appear to the right of the 'To' window to confirm it is signed. Click **Send** and the signed email is sent along with your digital ID. To sign a message in Outlook 2007 (or later), go to **Email Security** in the Trust Center (as above) and click on **Add digital signature to outgoing messages**.

If you receive a signed message like the one you have just sent, you will see a red ribbon by the message in the Inbox and also in the message window. When you open the message you will get some details in the form of a security help message. Clicking **Continue** brings up the message text or an error message if there is a problem with the message and it can not be trusted.

To send an encrypted message, you need a copy of your intended recipient's digital ID. You may already have this if they have previously sent you a digitally signed message, otherwise you can get it from the Certificate Authority that issued it by searching their website. Compose the message as you would normally then in Outlook Express® select **Tools→Encrypt** and a locked padlock will appear to the right of the To: window. When you click Send, Outlook Express® checks to see if it has a digital ID corresponding to the email address for the recipient and uses it to encrypt the message and attachments. In Outlook 2007, and later, this is done by

---

*MIME stands for Multi-purpose Internet Mail Extension and is the standard format for mail messages.

going to **Email Security** in the Trust Center (as above) and clicking on **Encrypt contents and attachments for outgoing messages**.

If you receive an encrypted message, then providing the sender has used your digital ID and you still have your private key, Outlook®/Outlook Express® automatically decrypts it and displays it. The padlock will be seen in the message window and the Inbox to show it was encrypted. You should also get a security help message to explain that the message was encrypted.

PGP

PGP stands for Pretty Good Privacy and is an alternative method of encrypting and signing emails. It is very popular in the security community. You need PGP software, but the good news is there are free versions available and versions that plug-in to Outlook® so that you can use your existing email tool for normal and encrypted email.

When you first run PGP you need to create a private key and choose a password to protect it. As we have already mentioned, this should be a strong password. You then have the option to register your public key with a PGP key holder to make sure it is available to people who want to send you encrypted email. Select **Edit→Copy** to put your public key into the clipboard, and then, after creating an email with Outlook®, just select **Edit→Paste** to paste it into the email. Send it to all the people you want to be able to send you confidential emails. If they want you to be able to send them encrypted emails (and they have PGP) they will reply with their public keys, which you need to add to your key chain. To do this, run PGP, or in Outlook® click the two keys icon. The way you send encrypted or signed messages will depend on the actual version of PGP you have running.

Hushmail

Hushmail is an example of web-based email. In web-based email, your email is delivered to and from a website rather than a private machine at your Internet Service Provider. Your web mail is typically protected by a password and username. Web mail has the advantage that you can log on from any internet access point anywhere in the world to get your mail. Hushmail is different to the well-known example, Hotmail and Gmail, in that it is encrypted. Most web email uses a web server to hold the email to and from the users. Hushmail is designed to ensure that only encrypted email is available on the web server and that only the sender and the recipient are able to read it. It is Hushmail's stated intention that they, the Hushmail providers, are not able to read any Hushmail users' encrypted email, despite the fact that they own and run the server. Hushmail uses the public key concept we discussed above so in order to send an encrypted email the sender needs the public key of the recipient.

To use Hushmail go to www.hushmail.com and follow the instructions for registration. You will create a private key by randomly moving your mouse and then you will choose a strong pass phrase to protect it. When you want to send an encrypted email to a fellow Hushmail user (remember this system is not compatible with the previous two encrypted examples) your message actually passes in encrypted form to the Hushmail website and is stored there until the recipient logs on and downloads it.

SPAM – JUNK EMAIL

'Spam, spam, spam, spam, spam and chips' – *Monty Python's Flying Circus*, circa 1968.

Spam is unwanted or unrequested email – junk email basically. The term originally came from users on News groups who decided they wanted to 'attack' a particular user they disliked. They sent 'flame' mail (mail criticising the user in no uncertain terms) and they sent a lot of it, much more than anyone could want. Hence 'spam', à la *Monty Python*. Later the term spam spread to refer to any unsolicited email. There are three main types of spam: commercial spam, chain letters and harassment.

Commercial spam

Commercial spam is unwanted or unrequested email trying to sell a product or service. Sometimes information of this type has been requested and sent legitimately, but cancelling it subsequently proves difficult. Bona fide companies will not want to sully their reputation by irritating their customers with too much email and so should accept requests to stop. What also sometimes happens is that when you register with a website, they require you to provide an email address. This address is sometimes used later for unsolicited adverts from that company or another company they may have sold their contacts database to. Always look out for a tick box that lets you state whether you are willing to accept email from a website or not. In many countries there is a legal requirement to allow the recipient to opt out of email communications. Less reputable companies and criminals may prove uncooperative, however. Common spam involves desperate attempts to sell branded items, jewellery and watches, cosmetic surgery and pharmaceuticals (both legal and illegal).

Chain letters

The second main type of spam is chain letters. These are emails that request the recipient to pass them on to their friends and contacts. Sometimes there are threats associated with them, sometimes there are promised benefits. Quite often they advertise 'Get rich quick' schemes. If you think such schemes exist, then you deserve these emails! If not you could try blocking them using the filter mechanism in your email software. Sometimes there is a supposed beneficiary who, if they actually existed, might well deserve our support. For example there is a chain email that has been going around for years that requests your support of a young boy with a serious illness who wants to break the world record for the number of get well cards received. Well the boy is now better, but his family cannot cope with all the email they continue to receive. The email continues to circulate and is now causing problems to the original beneficiary as well as irritating those who keep receiving it. It is good netiquette (internet etiquette) not to pass on chain email to others.

Another type of chain letter is the virus hoax. This is an email that purports to warn people of some terrible threat that could befall them if they do something that is probably quite safe. Naturally people want to warn their friends of this threat and so they pass the email on. But the threat does not exist and the hoax persists and propagates across cyberspace. If you suspect the warning to be true, then check out some of the respected places on the web that offer such information. If they have no information, then there is probably nothing to fear. A list of such places can be found in the section on virus hoaxes later in Chapter 6.

Email harassment

The third main type of spam is the worst. It is email that is personally directed harassment. It is sometimes malicious or abusive. It is the email equivalent of stalking and it can be quite distressing. It is certainly bad netiquette to send harassing emails, it is unnecessary and it can be illegal. If you receive anything like this make sure you keep the emails in case the situation gets worse and online harassment turns into physical harassment. Do reply at least once to put on record that you object to the nature of the communication and want it to stop. Do not keep replying because this may encourage the harasser. Report harassing emails to your employer if you believe it is coming from someone at work. People have been sacked for harassing colleagues in this way. If the email is threatening, then be prepared to call in the police. People have gone to jail for serious threats. Deal with harassment because it can sometimes escalate to become offensive phone calls or direct personal contact with the abuser.

Be aware that it is possible for someone to forge email and make it look like it came from someone else. An email harasser may try this to cover their tracks, but it is also possible for experts and the police to track such imposters down. Other forms of possible harassment that should be reported include the spreading of rumours, forged email or other online impersonation, and insulting postings on websites or newsgroups.

Basic precautions

In order to avoid many types of spam it is worth being cautious when giving out your email address. It is quite possible to own more than one email address. You can keep one for your family and friends and use others for commercial websites or newsgroups, or for communicating with strangers.

There are many providers of free email addresses. Why not register several email addresses and use one when there is a possibility of receiving spam. Using web-based email providers also means that spam does not reach your PC unless you want it to – you can just stop using that particular address or email site. A quick scan of the headers may show that the emails are spam and not worth downloading. There is a further benefit: using a variety of email addresses stops information about you being collated and referenced to a single address.

Alternatively, some ISPs forward your email regardless of the username, for example all email to any **username@my_email_address** may get sent to your home PC. So you can use any, and as many, usernames you like.

If there is the possibility that you are giving your email address where it might be used for spam, do not leave your usual email, leave a dummy such as **my-username+dodgy-site@my_email_address**, then if you get spam from 'dodgy-site' you can just filter and delete it as described later. You will also know which websites to avoid giving your business to.

If you find you need to provide an email address to a website, and you are certain you do not wish to receive any emails from that website, you could try this service from privacy.net (www.privacy.net). It allows you to use the address **me@privacy.net** (or **me** followed by any number, e.g. **me123@privacy.net**, if **me** is disallowed by the website). Privacy.net replies to all emails to these addresses with a standard message stating that the email was not requested and that it should be taken off their email list. This free service allows you to provide an email address in the safe and sure knowledge that no spam can reach you and no information about you is released.

Some spammers also 'harvest' accounts on web-based email that are sometimes machine generated. These spammer programs can also generate the addresses and send stuff to them (it doesn't really matter if they are unused addresses as long as some are live). A way of hiding your email address from such software harvesters is to write it as **my-nameNOSPAM@my-address**. A human being using your address will hopefully realise they should delete the words **NOSPAM**, but computer software may not.

A lot of spam can be automatically filtered by your ISP or by your email software. Outlook® 2007 and later, for example, will place any spam suspects in the 'Junk' folder. Note that if you find useful and legitimate email ending up here you will have to ensure the sender's email is added to the list of safe senders: Select **Actions→Junk E-mail→Add Sender to Safe Senders List**. Similarly, you can add an email that hasn't been recognised as spam, but in your opinion should be, by selecting **Action→Junk E-mail→Add Sender to Blocked Senders List**.

If you do receive spam and want to trace the culprit you can use the header of the email to track down the sender's ISP and complain. It is also worth complaining to your own ISP. In extreme circumstances they may block spammers. Try emailing your ISP at the address for reporting these sorts of problems. The address is often something like **abuse@yourISP**. You can also use some web services that help analyse email headers to find the sender. Senders can hide their tracks in the email itself. It's easy to fake a name and address for an email, but the header will still pick up the intermediary sites. Remember from the introduction to this chapter to use **File→Properties** to see the header details of a selected email.

One final tip to avoid spam. Some spam will ask you to reply if you want to have your name removed from a mailing list. Beware! This is sometimes a ruse to see if you are actually reading the mail from this mailing list. By replying, you are showing that your mailbox is 'live', and this may mean you get even more spam! On the other hand, reputable businesses will ensure that you can easily unsubscribe from mailing lists. You will have to decide whether your email is from a spammer or a bona fide business.

SUMMARY

- Email is an insecure means of communication. It is like a postcard, but one that can be forged.

- Never send confidential information, such as credit card numbers or social security numbers, by email.

- Never double-click on attachments. If you need to examine an attachment, then save the file by right-clicking it and selecting **Save**, and then run your (up-to-date) virus checker on the file. If in doubt return it to the sender.

- Configure Outlook®/Outlook Express® so that you are not giving away personal information and put it into the Restricted zone so that you can control security risks, such as ActiveX® and scripting.

- Choose an encryption tool (one that is also used by the people you want to communicate with) and set up a public/private key pair to send signed or encrypted email.

- Set up multiple email addresses to manage spam, either web-mail addresses or multiple aliases at your domain. Provide the aliases whenever there is a risk that the address could be used by spammers.

- Never reply to spam, especially to tell senders to stop sending it!

6 VIRUSES AND OTHER MALIGNANT SOFTWARE

A general term now widely used for all types of problem-causing software, some of which we have already discussed, is 'malware'. The term malware is usually quoted as originating from a contraction of 'malicious' and 'software', but given that a lot of software (including some viruses) has a nuisance value rather than a malicious intent, it might be better to think of it as 'malignant software'. According to my *Pocket Oxford English Dictionary*, malignant means 'harmful, showing intense ill-will, virulent', which is very apt. The prefix 'mal' is also often used just to mean bad. Malware is certainly bad software.

There is a lot of confusion over the terminology of malware and the precise definition of a virus. A virus is a program that makes copies of itself using a host file. A closely related program, known as a worm, can copy itself without attaching to another file. Both viruses and worms can carry malicious software with them, sometimes known as the payload. Some viruses and worms may not have a malicious intent, as is often assumed, but cause problems because they reproduce rapidly and clog up systems.

Despite their infamy, it seems that we still don't take viruses seriously enough. At one point it was found that 77 per cent of internet users did not update their anti-virus software regularly. Using and updating anti-virus software is the key countermeasure against malware. In the past this was difficult and time-consuming over dial-up internet connections, but now with broadband it is easy and, in theory, barely noticeable.

This chapter reviews the different types of malware and studies how they work in order that we can better understand what they do and better defend against them. It then looks at some major examples from the last few years. Countermeasures are covered, particularly the use of anti-virus software. Finally we look at what you can do if you do get infected, how to recognise what has happened and how to cure the infection. (Note that the term 'virus' and 'malware' are often used interchangeably.)

AN INTRODUCTION TO MALWARE

Malware is one of the major hazards that we face as a home computer user. It has been referred to as the common cold of modern technology. The main problem with viruses, and other malignant software, is that they spread, not through the air or from sneezing of course, but through the electrons of a digital connection.

The early viruses spread when people shared floppy disks, allowing the virus to copy itself on to a succession of new computers. Modern computer interactions are now much more complex, thanks to the internet, and viruses spread through email and software downloaded from websites and newsgroups. Viruses have become a very prominent manifestation of computer insecurity. One of the most virulent viruses was known as the Lovebug – at its peak it was believed to infect something like 1 in every 28 emails.

Viruses are basically pieces of software designed to be able to reproduce themselves with little human assistance. They can only infect your computer if you run an infected program, open an infected document or read an infected email. Like many other areas of security, there are no technological panaceas when it comes to viruses. It is in your interests to be aware of how viruses work, how they can infect you and what you can do if infected, as well as using the technical measures at your disposal to prevent them.

The principal way to prevent a virus infection is by scanning files for its tell-tale presence. This is how anti-virus software works. To do this requires the scanning program to know what the virus is like in order to have something to compare it against. So when a new virus is found, all the anti-virus scanners (on all the millions of machines worldwide) have to be updated with the unique characteristics of the new virus, and of course this takes time. The faster the virus spreads, the harder it is to get anti-virus software updated in time.

Viruses are not just impersonal attacks on a machine. Some can be far more insidious. They can leave behind what is known as a back door, or remote access program, to your computer, which can allow an attacker to take over your PC. There are many such back door programs and viruses are one of the main ways of getting them on to a victim's machine. Once there, they can monitor the keyboard for passwords or credit card numbers, monitor the microphone or webcam, or use your internet connection for their own nefarious ends.

The first viruses could only infect executable software. Once an infected program was run, the virus attempted to infect other programs in the same way as the original. The infected software may even appear to run perfectly normally, thus hiding the nature of the infection. The virus may, however, perform additional activities through what is known as a payload, and it is the payload that generally determines exactly what effect the virus has on your system.

More recently, some software applications took on the ability to run certain types of code called scripts. Virus writers learnt how to use these scripts to attach viruses to the files, such as word-processing documents, that harboured the scripts.

Why do people write viruses? It seems that viruses are written by the same sort of people who become criminal hackers, and for the same sorts of reasons. Virus writers may be pranksters or malicious vandals. They may be bored, introverted, computer-obsessed individuals looking to demonstrate their technical prowess. Others may have a fair degree of computer knowledge, but have a point to make, such as wanting to attack a specific company or piece of software. Some write a virus to become famous or infamous. Other viruses may be written by novices (there are virus construction kits available on the internet) or by experts performing experiments, but such experiments can go wrong and once a virus is distributed the author has no control over it.

Perhaps the most famous case is the original internet worm launched by Robert Morris in 1988, before the internet was the global commercial entity it is today. The internet was basically closed for many days as copies of the worm continued to multiply and choke up the available bandwidth. It took a lot of detective work by some very skilled people to understand what was going on and get things back to normal. Virus writing is a crime in many countries and some people have been imprisoned for it. Robert Morris received a fine of over $10,000 and community service.

If you are lucky you may catch a virus that does nothing more than copy itself onward and leave nothing behind. If you are unlucky, you may have a virus that wipes your hard disk (have you backed up recently?) or, in the case of a virus called CIH, may even require you to change a piece of hardware.

Nowadays, many file formats are vulnerable to virus infection. There are more than 50,000 known viruses and every month sees a new major infection. Virus infections are also becoming more virulent. The first macro virus, released in 1995, took four months to become the most prevalent virus. In 1999, Melissa, an email-enabled macro virus took four days. In 2000, Loveletter took just five hours. It has been postulated that a world-wide internet infection could be achieved in a matter of minutes.

TYPES OF MALWARE

Malware comes in many shapes and sizes. It propagates in various ways and subjects our PCs to differing degrees of damage.

Viruses and worms
Stealth viruses try to hide from the operating system, from the user and from anti-virus software. Here are the main types of virus according to how they work.

Macro viruses
Macro viruses take advantage of the fact that modern office software can be controlled by small programs known as scripts or macros, which are embedded in the files the applications use. Macros are not by any means inherently bad. You can create your own macros to perform operations you wish to repeat frequently and save yourself time spent in going through each individual instruction of the operation. However, macros can be made into quite complex programs. Microsoft® software, such as Word and Excel®, contains macros that can be programmed in Visual Basic for Applications® (VBA). A VBA macro might gain access to email addresses stored in an address book and use them as a way of emailing itself over the internet. Thanks mainly to this ability, macro viruses are now the most common type of virus.

File viruses

A file virus is a virus that attaches itself to a program. File viruses do not infect other types of file, such as documents. When the infected program file is run, the virus part lodges itself in the computer's memory and subsequently may infect all programs run afterwards.

Boot sector viruses

Whereas file viruses infect copies of programs, a boot sector virus works by infecting a special part of a disk, the boot sector. Both floppy and hard disks have a boot sector that tells the computer how to read the disk. The boot sector can also contain a program, the boot program, which contains enough of the PC operating system to start the computer without having to resort to starting the whole system. Boot programs are usually used on floppy drives and serve as a back-up in case the main operating system is corrupted or otherwise misbehaving. A virus infecting a boot program will be run before any other program on the system, including the operating system itself, and thus gets free rein to do what it wants and replicate itself to other programs.

Worms

A worm has the ability to copy itself and travel across a network or the internet. A worm does not attach itself to other programs although it may use them (such as an email client) to propagate. In itself it is not malicious but, as with viruses, it can carry a destructive payload.

Trojan horses

A Trojan horse is so-called after the famous wooden horse that the Greeks used to deceive the city of Troy. A Trojan horse program similarly does something unexpected. A particularly problematic example is the Remote Access Trojan (or RAT) of which there are many. These programs set up your PC to be remotely controlled from across the internet. Well-known past examples include Back Orifice 2000, Remote Explorer, Netbus and SubSeven. Trojan horses often turn up in shareware and pirated software downloaded from the internet.

Mobile code

Mobile code is a special type of program that can be downloaded from a website by a browser and run on the browser's machine. Mobile code is often used to make web pages more dynamic, for example with sound effects and moving graphics. For this reason it is sometimes also known as active content. We have mentioned mobile code such as Java®, JavaScript®, Visual Basic® script and ActiveX® in Chapter 4.

Mobile code generally has some form of built-in security mechanism to make it more secure than downloading a standard executable. JavaScript®, for example, cannot access local system resources, Java® has constraints on what it can access. ActiveX® has no such constraints and is the most serious problem with mobile code. ActiveX® can access files on the system it is running and even set up network connections.

Spyware and adware

Spyware is software that sends personal information about you over the internet without your permission or knowledge. There are two ways in which spyware operates: one is as part of the browser and the other is as a standalone piece of software that you may have downloaded or picked up some other way. Your browser can give out a lot if information about you as we saw in Chapter 4. Standalone spyware can be even worse, monitoring your PC activities more widely and reporting back what it finds, such as passwords you have typed.

Adware is nuisance software that puts up extra banner ads and pop-up windows with advertisements. It can be similar to spyware in that can monitor what you do on the PC and use this to determine what sort of adverts to display.

Miscellaneous malware
Keylogger
A covert program that records your typing in an attempt to steal passwords, credit card numbers or other data. It is typically left behind as a payload and can communicate over the internet to send the key presses it has detected.

Drive-by downloads
These are programs that download surreptitiously to your PC automatically whilst you browse a particular web page. They do not inform the user that they have done so or what they do. They can be surprisingly common and new variants are often posted on to legitimate websites or hosted and distributed on popular social networking sites.

Data diddlers
Data diddlers are an insidious type of malware. They alter data files, such as spreadsheets and databases, but they make small changes so that it can be difficult to detect whether a file has actually been altered. Consequently if such a program is discovered, the integrity of all data on the system comes into question. Fortunately, there are few examples to date of data diddlers that have had a widespread impact.

Logic and time bombs
Bombs usually refer to malware with a distinctly damaging intent. Logic bombs cause the damage when they are set off by some specific happening or logical event. Time bombs will go off on a particular date or at a particular time and will otherwise lie dormant. Often, time bombs are set to go off at some sort of anniversary, for example the Chernobyl virus that is activated each year on 26 April, the date of the Chernobyl nuclear disaster.

Home page hijackers
Your browser's home page can be redirected to a specific website by malware. Home page hijackers are often used to direct home pages to pornographic websites and can make sure that even if you reset the home page, they hijack it again when the PC starts up. If you get this problem the first step is to attempt to revert to the previous home page. In Internet Explorer® use **Tools→Internet Options→Programs→Reset web settings** (if available in your version). If this doesn't work, you may need to search for, and install, a specific utility to eliminate the problem.

Rogue diallers
This malware attempts to hijack the dial-up of your web browser so that instead of dialling your ISP it calls a premium rate number. Not only can this be embarrassing, but it can also be costly. Unlike some security problems these costs are not

written off and calls are charged for by the telecoms company. Some people have found they have incurred over £1000 in call charges. This problem only affects users of dial-up internet connections and not broadband. Always check the phone number being dialled is the one you expect it to be and if you need to change it or are asked to change it make sure it is genuine.

SOME MALWARE EXAMPLES

It is worthwhile looking at some specific examples of malware to see what they can do and how they do it, in the hope it gives you some understanding of the risks you are exposed to and to re-enforce the need to take appropriate countermeasures. Bear in mind that most of these examples have effectively 'died-out' because they are old and recognised by anti-virus software and now fail to propagate. You may be unlikely to get these specific infections, but very similar malware still circulates.

Viruses and worms
Melissa
Melissa went beyond the normal reproduction mechanisms of macro viruses. Instead of just infecting Word documents as they were opened on an infected PC, it used a program written in VBA, the macro programming language, to send itself in an attachment file to the first 50 entries in a user's address book. This emailing was done in the background, unbeknownst to the user. A recipient who opened the attachment would become infected and could immediately send Melissa out to 50 more people. This chain reaction enabled Melissa to spread around the world in four days. Although there was no destructive payload, the sheer number of messages clogged up many company email systems. In many people's eyes the worm had turned!

BubbleBoy
Before BubbleBoy, users were comforted to know that it was not possible to catch a virus just by reading email. BubbleBoy was written to demonstrate that this was not necessarily true. The author sent it to anti-virus researchers who were warned of the possible consequences, but it then started to spread. It used a vulnerability in ActiveX® to allow it to run automatically if the email that contained it was read. The Preview pane in Outlook®/Outlook Express® is, in effect, reading the email, so users with the Preview pane enabled were infected with no action on their part. Microsoft® released a patch for the ActiveX® hole, but many people feel that the Preview pane is a benefit that is not worth the risk.

Caligula
This is a macro virus that attempts to steal a PGP user's private key by looking for PGP in the file system and searching for the default name of the key ring. This malware acted as a warning for encryption users everywhere. Even if you could use perfect encryption, so strong that no one could break it, it is insecure if someone has a copy of your private key. This virus showed how attackers might try to grab users' private keys.

ILoveYou or The Love Letter
In 2000, this macro worm spread even faster than Melissa had the previous year, covering the world in just a few hours. It propagated in almost the same way as

Melissa in that it required the user to double-click on an attachment and then it sent itself to people in the address list. Unfortunately it was destructive; it overwrote files; redirected Internet Explorer®'s home page and tried to download another file to steal passwords. One variant even tried to steal online banking information from PCs that used internet banking at the United Bank of Switzerland. The interesting thing about IloveYou was that it used a form of social engineering to get people to open the attachment. Even people who knew better and would never normally double-click on an attachment were tricked. The virus arrived with the subject 'Kindly check the attached LOVELETTER coming from me' and an attachment named 'LOVE-LETTER-FOR-YOU.TXT.VBS'. This was just too tempting and many people double-clicked out of curiosity.

SST

SST is also known as the Anna Kournikova virus. It arrives as an email with an apparent JPEG file attachment, which the email claims is a picture of Anna Kournikova, the tennis player. It was not in fact a JPEG file but a VB script that disguises itself by using a double dot extension **.jpg.vbs**. Outlook® only displayed the **.jpg** and hid the **.vbs** extension. Coupled with intense interest in Ms Kournikova, this tricked many people into double-clicking on the attachment.

Klez

One variant of Klez could select random names from an address book to use as the sender address, thereby disguising itself as a genuine email. It also used a large range of subject, body text and attachment names to avoid easy recognition. It could even disable some anti-virus programs.

BadTrans

This worm propagated, like the BubbleBoy example, when an infected email was opened. It exploited a vulnerability in Outlook®. Its claim to fame is that it propagated by sending replies to emails in a victim's Inbox and attaching itself to the message. That way the new recipients could easily mistake it as a genuine reply. BadTrans also installed a Trojan horse and then attempted to email the IP address of the infected machine to the virus author. The Trojan ran a keylogging program that can record all keyboard typing including passwords and credit card numbers.

Sasser

Sasser was a self-executing worm that travelled over the internet by exploiting a flaw in Windows® XP and Windows® 2000. It did not use email, but located vulnerable systems that it could infect using a direct network connection. It controlled infected machines to look for, and infect, further machines. It became quite notorious because it affected a number of high-profile organisations, such as the Taiwanese post office and the UK coastguard.

Trojan horses
Back Orifice (BO2K)

This is a remote access Trojan, one of the most popular for two reasons. Firstly the source code has been distributed freely along with a software development kit, allowing programmers of a hacking disposition to modify and improve it. Secondly, it is highly flexible and comes with a graphical user interface for the 'user' to set parameters, such as how it communicates between the server (running on the unsuspecting host) and the client.

BO2K has a range of options for the potential intruder, including keystroke logging, microphone and webcam spying, password dumping, message sending and remote reboot and lock-up. BO2K is an example of malware that runs stealthily on a PC: it will not appear as a task in the task list (when you simultaneously press the Ctrl + Alt + Del keys). BO2K has no capability to move from PC to PC. It could be a payload for a virus or worm, but, because it is well known, it will be spotted by anti-virus software. It has become the prototype of a range of Trojan horse malware. The main protection from this class of threat, apart from keeping your anti-virus utility up to date, is to ensure your firewall is on and blocking outgoing traffic.

Win32.Qaz
Qaz has a distinct claim to fame. Some years ago, the Microsoft® Corporation reported that it had been found inside its company servers and may have been there some months. It was reported that new versions of Microsoft® software had been stolen by the Trojan. It showed the world that even the biggest corporations were not immune to the hacker threat.

MALWARE COUNTERMEASURES

As with every security risk described in this book, the standard measures we have discussed are also applicable to defence against viruses. Back-ups will help you recover from a successful attack, patched software will reduce the risk from viruses that exploit security flaws in your software, and awareness of what, and what not, to do is very important.

The first thing to remember is to avoid double-clicking on attachments to emails or instant messages. This is the primary way that viruses are spread today. If you do need to run a program received by email or downloaded from the web, then take the following precautions. Save the file (right click it, but do not open it) into a blank folder and scan it with your anti-virus software. Even if the scanner gives the all clear you should contact the sender to check that it was sent to you deliberately and that the contents are benign. Never open a suspect attachment without scanning with an up-to-date anti-virus product. Anti-virus software is the main countermeasure to malware.

The prevalence and risk of viruses is so great that a whole industry has grown selling anti-virus software, and there is a large range of software to choose from. Additionally, there are web services that perform a virus scan on your machine from across the internet. These should be used to complement mainstream anti-virus software in case you are not running your anti-virus software properly, you haven't been able to download the latest signature file or upgrade (they can be quite large, often many megabytes) or in the extreme case of a virus turning off your anti-virus software.

Using anti-virus software
Anti-virus software generally works in a very straightforward way. It keeps a database that holds information about every virus it knows about. Each virus has a signature: a unique string of computer code. The anti-virus software checks files on your computer against its database of signatures to try and detect a virus. If a new virus appears that is not in the database, then the software simply will not

find it. That is why it is absolutely vital that you update the signature database for your anti-virus software regularly.

The rate of release of new viruses is so high and new viruses are spreading so quickly that updating your anti-virus software is probably your most critical security activity. It is critical to update it every time you log on to the internet. Anti-virus software should check for updates as soon as you connect to the internet, which saves you the bother of remembering.

After updating, the next most important aspect of anti-virus software is config-uration. There are usually many different ways to configure and run anti-virus software. The safest way is to regularly scan all files on your PC, to scan files whenever they are accessed by applications and to scan downloaded files (including, and especially, emails) as soon as they are downloaded.

Understanding how to configure some anti-virus software can be quite difficult. You will probably need to look at the manual or online help documents to make sure you are getting the best from your particular anti-virus software. Make sure you know how to use the various features and can figure out the following:

- How to get different types of files examined.
- How to get emails (and other internet downloads) checked when downloaded.
- How to perform updates.
- How to ensure background scanning is activated.
- How to automate the running of full scans periodically.

You can test anti-virus software with the Eicar test file available from their website www.eicar.org. Eicar is an organisation working to counter malware. The test file is not a virus. It is a benign file, and all the vendors of anti-virus software have agreed to recognise it. If your software recognises it (say in an email), then you have some confidence that your software is scanning your email correctly.

It is recommended to keep abreast of malware developments because of the dangers from malware and the rate at which they are evolving. This can help you to under-stand any new risks. There are many websites devoted to fighting malware. You can also subscribe to an alert service, which gives you an update on the malware threat and any particular actions you should take. For example there may be a new virus 'in the wild' that is exploiting a specific vulnerability. If your PC has that vulnerability, then depending on the seriousness of the virus you may wish to patch that vulnerability sooner rather than later.

Anti-virus software is only as good as the last update. It is easy to be over-confi-dent. Anti-virus software can also give false positives: that is it thinks a virus is present when actually it isn't there. This can be difficult to resolve. If your anti-virus software does indicate the presence of a virus, then your next step is to attempt to eradicate it. This is dealt with later in this chapter. If you follow the procedures for eradication, but the software still suggests a virus is present, then you may well have a false positive. If your PC is running normally and there doesn't seem to be any anomalous activity, then you shouldn't be too concerned. Check with the software vendor to see if this is a known problem or search the web for any other suggestions on eradication, just in case the initial action has not sufficed.

In performing virus scans, anti-virus software has to interfere and interrupt the usual way your computer operates. Sometimes this can have negative consequences and in the worst case it could cause your machine to crash. After setting up the software, check for odd behaviour (e.g. the virus scanner may be excessively slowing down your PC). If you do encounter problems try reconfiguring the software in various ways to see if they go away. You may have to stop full scans running in the background, but you can maintain a level of security by periodically running them manually.

Choosing anti-virus software

Anti-virus software is very important to your PC security, so it is worthwhile thoroughly researching different products before purchase. Look for reviews on the web or in magazines. Look out for products that automatically update your virus signatures when you go online. Other factors you need to check out are the reputation of the vendor. A well-known vendor may have more resources available to monitor virus threats and issue updates rapidly. Good free software is available, such as the AVG Anti-virus free edition (www.avg.com) and Microsoft®'s Security Essentials, amongst others. A guide to free anti-virus software is available at www.freebyte.com/antivirus.

Good information on tests of anti-virus products is available at:

- www.av-test.org
- www.virusbtn.com

Other malware security software

As well as using standard anti-virus products (which can usually also detect Trojans), there is a range of specifically anti-Trojan software, which can be used to clean up your system after a Trojan infection. They can detect and eliminate Trojan horses and even fix some of the changes the Trojan may have made to your files, such as to the Windows® Registry. Some of these products are free. The programs need updating just like anti-virus products. It is not feasible to give a definitive list of products because their numbers and capabilities change regularly, so search carefully on the internet for as many independent recommendations as you can before using any.

Microsoft® also supplies Windows® Defender with Windows Vista® and Windows® 7 (it can be downloaded for Windows® XP). If you think that your anti-virus software is not detecting spyware or if you want a second opinion, then you can switch on Windows® Defender (you can go offline and temporarily switch off your anti-virus utility).

RECOGNISING AND CURING VIRUS INFECTIONS

The best, and quickest, way to recognise that your computer has a virus infection is by being warned by your anti-virus software. If for some reason this doesn't happen, then you may get other indications that your PC is infected, such as slow running, problems with some of your software, alerts from your firewall or unusual system messages.

Prevention is definitely better than cure, but if your PC does succumb to a virus infection, what should you do? This will depend very much on the type of virus. If your anti-virus software can identify the virus, then you have a headstart in finding how to eliminate it. In many cases it will almost certainly be possible to find a cure, although if the malware has already executed there may be permanent damage, which is why back-ups are important. The anti-virus vendors publish the steps to take on their websites.

If the virus has activated, then things become much harder. The virus may have caused some problems with your data; it may still be lurking to cause you even more problems at a later date. Firstly, don't panic! It is quite possible to do more damage trying to cure a virus than the virus actually did. In order to start work disinfecting your PC you will need to boot it up cleanly.

It is not usually sufficient simply to delete the virus and reboot the PC. Neither, in many cases, will reformatting the hard disk be very helpful. When the PC starts, it looks in the boot sector of the hard drive to locate the operating system. A common trait of a virus is to hide in the boot sector where it is not seen by the operating system and so is not subject to formatting. The virus can get control of the PC before your operating system and so will reappear.

Most anti-virus tool vendors produce tools to disinfect certain viruses. Further advice and information can be obtained from websites such as http://getvirushelp.com and www.antivirusworld.com.

VIRUS HOAXES

Computer viruses are real and there are plenty of them. Even so, some people seem to need to make up stories about them and imagine viruses that do not exist. Welcome to the virus hoax. A virus hoax is a fictitious report or warning of a non-existent virus. This can be very frustrating and time wasting.

Just like in the real world with a bomb hoax, it might be difficult to tell the difference between a hoax and the real thing. People sometimes respond as if it were true and the virus actually existed. A network manager believing the hoax might shut down the network causing the same impact on the organisation as a real virus might have done. Even if such a major response is avoided, a widely spread hoax can take up network bandwidth. A virus hoax can spread, you guessed it, by email. The more credible and scary the story, the wider the hoax circulates. Everyone who receives a virus hoax wastes their time just in reading it.

Perhaps things wouldn't be too bad if this was a rare occurrence, but there are hundreds of virus hoax emails doing the rounds. If you receive a virus warning, consider whether it is a hoax before taking any action. Hoaxes generally have three characteristics:

- They have an amateurish and panic-stricken style, often claiming that the virus is the worst ever found, cannot be stopped and will destroy everything, or words to that effect.

- They may invent some organisation that has announced or found this virus, or they may claim the government or some official body is warning people about it.

- They entreat you to pass the message on to as many of your friends as possible. This is similar to a chain letter. It is why the hoax spreads and is why you received it in the first place.

What should we do if we receive what looks like a hoax virus warning? First of all there is no need to react immediately: if there really is a problem there are professionals who will deal with it. We can check whether the warning is real by visiting a website dedicated to fighting viruses or tracking virus hoaxes. There are malware hoax databases at www.itsecurityportal.com and www.vmyths.com.

You could also check informally with friends (i.e. not by email) whether they know anything. Unless there is very compelling evidence it is best to kill the hoax by not forwarding it any further. Don't send out virus warnings to all your friends unless you are sure it has come from a reputable source and that your friends need to know urgently. If not, hold fire and stop clogging up other people's mailboxes.

The danger with hoaxes is that when someone cries wolf too many times we stop responding. If we see, and disbelieve, a lot of hoaxes, we may become complacent to the real threat and find ourselves disbelieving a genuine warning.

Scareware
Scareware is a particular kind of hoax used as a scam. It is an attempt to convince you that there is a virus on your machine and that you need to pay for specific security software to clear it up. In June 2011, it was reported that the FBI had led worldwide arrests of a gang that had made tens of millions of dollars from such a fraud. Many different variants of this scam exist, but usually the aim is to scare the user and convince them there is something seriously wrong with their computer. A hoax message may appear via a website or the attackers may have managed to get malicious software onto your PC. Unlike most malware its main purpose is to extort you into buying a cure.* If you do, then the criminals pocket the money and may gain access to your credit card details. Of course there are legitimate tools to use to clean virus infections, but these would never initiate the clean-up process. Any unusual recommendation for purchasing anything for any reason should be considered sceptically. Check using a web search to see if there are any reports of similar scams.

---

*You may even receive a phone call attempting a similar ruse, such as that your computer has a virus problem.

SUMMARY

- Viruses and other malignant software are one of the biggest risks for home PC users. The main way they are spread is through email attachments, although any file obtained from memory sticks, instant messaging, social networking or chat rooms should be treated with caution.

- The principal countermeasure is anti-virus software. This must be configured carefully and use up-to-date virus signatures. Make sure you understand what checks the software is performing and when it is performing them.

- Use a product that updates your anti-virus signatures regularly and as soon as you access the internet. Check from time to time that it is running correctly and is up to date.

- There are many species of malware. Viruses and worms can have malicious payloads. Remote access Trojans can make your PC a slave of the person controlling the Trojan. Use personal firewall software to block outbound Trojans.

- Cleaning up after an infection can be tricky and varies from virus to virus. You will need to check your anti-virus software vendor's website for help or search the internet carefully for trustworthy advice.

- Virus hoaxes should be ignored. Never forward them to friends or colleagues. Be cautious of any attempts to sell you security software, especially if related to suspicious or unusual PC behaviour. Check on the web if you are unsure about anything or if you feel you may need to take some action. In general the best you can do is to update your anti-virus software and carry on as usual.

7 WORKING SECURELY AT HOME

Many people nowadays do some work at home. They may work on their home PC with data they have brought from work on a memory card. They may connect to their work computers over the internet or dial in directly. They may use their employer's laptops to work at home or when away. They may have a small business that they run from home. A number of security issues arise when work and home computing mix.

So far through this book we have looked at protecting our own information. In this chapter we recognise that working at home means we have a responsibility to protect other people's data and systems: namely those of our employer, our employees, colleagues, customers and clients.

RISKS AT HOME

Let us assume that you are taking the security measures described in this book. There are some additional risks to your work when at home that you should pay particular attention to.

Personnel security
Children can be a risk to our data. The problem comes not so much from teenage super-hackers, but from toddlers with roving fingers! They can switch off computers, type over our data, delete files. We need some limited access control to keep them at bay. Use password protected logins and a screen saver. Young children also do not understand how equipment should be looked after. A CD is a nice wheel! A PC tower is a very useful table on which to rest a cup of milk! If toddler 'vandals' are at large, then make sure the screen saver's time interval for activation is short, or lock the door to your office when you go for a drink or to the washroom.

Physical security
A lock on the office door also protects against theft. From time to time, PCs become attractive items for the average thief. If the thief is put off by a lock and just takes your hi-fi and jewellery, then you have one less thing to worry about. At least valuable items can be insured. Valuable information can be almost invaluable. Companies can go bust if they lose a lot of essential data. PCs at home can be targets for thieves for other reasons too. Corporate espionage is big business. If you are a senior executive you are a potential target. If you work in a sensitive area, say for the government, you are a potential target.

Technical security

One way of defending against data theft is by encrypting your data (see Chapter 2).

Another risk is from cordless phones. If your PC connects to the internet through a modem, and you have a cordless phone connected to the same line, then it might surprise you to learn that even when you are not actually using the phone, its base station is still transmitting. It does not have an on/off switch. Although it is a fairly unlikely occurrence, tapping into a cordless phone provides a cheap and simple way of listening in to your modem data traffic. Consequently anything sent 'in the clear' to or from the internet or to or from your company network may be being broadcast by your cordless phones base station. If you think you are at risk from corporate espionage it is worthwhile disconnecting the phone whilst you are online.

Several notorious cases have shown that it is also possible to intercept mobile phone calls. If you are really worried about this you can buy phones that run strong encryption between compatible handsets.

TELECOMMUTING

Most companies have a computer security policy. You must read it carefully, and make special note of any conditions regarding working from home. This is not just for the company's benefit. If you were to infringe the rules laid out in the company policy you are potentially putting yourself at risk of dismissal. For your own good, make a note of any parts of the policy that are relevant to you and especially those relevant to working at home or use of a company laptop.

If you work for a medium or large company, there will undoubtedly be a set of security measures in place: a firewall to restrict access to and from the internet; anti-virus software on every desktop that is remotely and regularly updated; filtering software at the gateway to provide content protection; automated overnight back-ups; and possibly many more. Your work network may use operating systems such as Windows® NT, WindowsServer® or versions of UNIX®, which allow better access control than most home PCs. Once you work at home you are potentially bypassing these security measures and the employer has no means to check your level of home security. The remote site, the home, can become a vulnerable access point to the corporate network.

No company is immune to the risks from home users. In early 2001, Microsoft® reported that their network had been hacked into and that the source code for some of their software may have been accessed. The route for this hacker was via a Microsoft® employee accessing his work computer remotely. Responsible employees should take information security measures as specified by their company and outlined in this book.

LAPTOPS AND SMARTPHONES

Laptops, netbooks, smartphones and the like allow us to make our computing power and our data mobile. This brings additional risks because there is much more potential for them to be lost or stolen than a desktop system.

One of the major risks is the theft of a laptop, especially when travelling and at places such as stations and airports. A common way to steal a laptop is at an airport X-ray screening area. After putting your laptop on the conveyor belt someone gets in your way and starts to delay you through the metal detector. Meanwhile an accomplice picks up your laptop on the other side and disappears with it.

Another example is the risk of theft from a car. At the very least a laptop should be locked out of sight. There are, however, examples of thieves lurking at places, such as motorway service stations, where many laptop owners can be seen locking their laptops securely in the boot of their car when they go for lunch. The thieves then strike knowing that the owners will probably be away for sufficient time for them to unobtrusively break in to the boot.

There are a few lessons we should learn from the risk of theft:

- Keep your laptop or mobile device with you at all times.
- Delete unneeded files.
- Back up often.
- Do not store sensitive data on portable devices.
- Make sure that you have password protection enabled where possible.
- Consider the use of hard disk encryption.

A thief will probably be more interested in formatting the hard disk in order to sell the laptop than in looking through your files, but it is best to be safe with your data. If you are a senior executive you may have information of interest to a rival company on your PC. If you are a scientist you may have information about unpublished research or confidential patent information. Guard your information well. In general it's best not to store personal information on laptops; information such as tax details, financial files, CV etc. will give too much detail to a thief and may allow your identity to be stolen.

Some commercial products track stolen laptops if they are subsequently used to log on to the internet. They can be configured to send an alert.

SMALL OFFICE AND HOME OFFICE NETWORKS

What if you are your employer? Or what if you are part of a small business with a small IT network or have a small PC network at home? Network security is a much bigger topic than the PC security issues discussed in this book. You may have to take some responsibility for network security.

Note that a survey found that over 90 per cent of workers felt they had no part to play in preventing the spread of viruses and around two thirds will forward spam to friends and colleagues without thinking. An alarming number were unaware of basic security measures, such as not double-clicking on attachments to thwart viruses. The problem of awareness is clearly very important and the key messages outlined in this book should be made known to all users of your network.

Many of the relevant measures are introduced in this book and they easily extend to a network infrastructure. Technical steps include:

- Instigate a regular back-up of the system whether or not each individual user makes back-ups. A back-up could save your company from extinction.

- Make sure your users have some security awareness (buy them a copy of this book!), and make sure they use good passwords and read the security policy etc.

- Have someone responsible for security, if not you. Enforce patching and updating software and keep good records of security actions.

- Anti-virus tools will need to be up to date on everyone's desktop and used to scan incoming emails. Microsoft® Security Essentials is (at time of writing) available free for small businesses with up to 10 PCs as long as you are running genuine licensed versions of Windows®.

- A firewall of some sort should separate any internal network from the internet. You will need to understand how to configure and use a firewall. The most important point is to ensure that any unnecessary services are blocked.

- Microsoft® have a free tool for download known as the Microsoft® Baseline Security Analyzer (MBSA). It scans your Microsoft® software for configuration weaknesses and checks that you are up to date with software patches (rather like Windows® Update, but for a wider range of applications). MBSA is a free tool that helps small- and medium-sized businesses determine their security state in accordance with Microsoft® security recommendations. It also offers remediation guidance. It can detect common administrative vulnerabilities and missing security updates on your computers.

Quick tip: Do not get too dependent on a single member of staff to look after your IT. Should something happen to them or they fall out with you, you are putting all your data at risk. The insider attack is one of the biggest risks facing businesses. You do have to trust people, especially in a small business, but make sure trust is not blind and does not turn into reliance and dependence.

Company security policy

An appointed manager should write a security policy for a company IT system. This is to ensure that all staff know what the company expects of them and gives the company a basis for disciplining anyone who contravenes the policy. It should start from a risk assessment and cover the various countermeasures discussed in this book. In addition staff should:

- know who their security point of contact is;

- be advised to consult the point of contact or check on the internet if they think they have a problem, before spreading alarm;

- report security problems as soon as possible to the security point of contact.

As well being aware of the security policy, users should be clear about how they are expected to use the internet. This is known as an acceptable use policy. It should cover such things as what private use of the internet is permitted (e.g. personal browsing, accessing social networking websites) and the avoidance of content that might cause offence to co-workers.

Be aware that if you use personal firewalls or other security software for business purposes, then you will need to check the licence conditions and pay for them if appropriate. Some software that may be free for use at home may not be free if used for business purposes. If this is the case, please pay the appropriate fee and follow the terms of your licence. You may appreciate the support and extra features that sometimes come with the paid-for version. Note also that directors of companies in the UK using illegal unlicensed software can go to prison for up to two years, with an unlimited fine.

If you want to access home office PCs from the internet whilst out of the office, you will need to take extra care. You can install programs that give you complete access and remote control of your PC, such as PC Anywhere and GotoMyPC. However, these programs do provide the potential for an intruder to also access your PC, for example by breaking your password. If you need this capability, it is essential you give security a high profile and install a good firewall.

Finally, many attacks are by insiders: employees, ex-employees, temporary employees. If you employ anyone in any capacity, then be careful how much you trust them with your PCs and the data. When anyone leaves, for whatever reason, or if relations turn sour with anyone with access to your systems, change the passwords and make sure your back-ups are extra safe.

Disaster recovery and business continuity

Disaster recovery is often seen as something that only large companies need to prepare for, but it can also apply to small companies. If your IT facilities fail, how could you keep your business running? You need to answer this question and plan for this contingency.

CYBERCRIME AND THE LAW

First of all let's dispel an internet myth. The internet is not lawless. Many people seem to believe that existing laws do not apply to the internet. This is false. Many laws apply and have been used in court cases. There are quite a few laws, in various countries, that relate to computer security and they are worth a little discussion to see whether they help or hinder us in our home-working activities.

However, there are a number of difficulties when applying the law to computers and internet activities in general. One is that the internet observes no national boundaries. A crime could be committed in one country against victims in another using computers located in a third. Does the victim have to use the laws of a foreign country to get a prosecution and, perhaps, some redress? Another problem is that the law enforcement operations in each of these countries will have to cooperate to find the perpetrator, gather evidence and make a convincing case to a court. This is difficult enough, but the laws in different countries can be very different and what might seem like a crime in one country may be perfectly legal in another. The law, on its own, has a limited role in stopping internet crime and maintaining computer security for four main reasons:

- Cybercrimes often have an international dimension.

- The technologies are changing fast, and novel crimes are emerging, which means there is only a small amount of relevant case law.

- Difficulties in investigating and finding sufficient evidence to successfully prosecute perpetrators.

- The impact of the crime, and therefore its seriousness, can be difficult to assess.

One point worth noting is that businesses can be held liable for the data on employees PCs. The acceptable use policy, mentioned above, is very important in demonstrating the company's attempts to ensure users use their company PCs appropriately.

Computer law in the UK

Some new laws have also been passed to address specific concerns. The following is an outline of the main scope of some of the most relevant laws. Please get qualified legal advice if you have any questions about your legal obligations.

Copyright issues

Most offences in relation to copyright are civil offences, and therefore require legal action to be instigated by the owner of the copyright that is being violated. Certain large-scale operations, however, such as the bulk copying of computer software, can be prosecuted as a criminal offence under the Copyright, Designs and Patents Act (1988).

The Data Protection Act (1998)

This Act concerns the collection, processing, use and disclosure of information about identifiable individuals. The aim of the Data Protection Act is twofold. Firstly, it gives rights to individuals about whom information is held. Secondly, it places obligations on those who handle personal data. One of the main obligations is to register with the Information Commissioner. It is also necessary to inform individuals, on request, what information you hold on them.

As a small business you are likely to hold information on customers, employees, suppliers, clients or other members of the public. If you hold this kind of information (whether it's on paper, in data files or on a website) the Data Protection Act (1998) applies to you. If you hold personal information of any kind about a living person you must comply with the Data Protection Act, whether you need to register with the Information Commissioner or not.

The eight principles of good information handling are contained in the Act. It specifies that personal information is:

- processed fairly and lawfully;
- processed for limited purposes;

- adequate, relevant and not excessive;
- accurate and up to date;
- not kept for longer than is necessary;
- processed in line with the rights of individuals;
- secure;
- not transferred to other countries without adequate protection.

The definition of processing is wide and covers virtually any action carried out on a computer. This includes obtaining, recording, holding, processing and analysing personal information. The Information Commissioner can take out enforcement action to ensure your information processing is in line with these principles, so you should ensure your internal procedures accommodate these data handling requirements, and you must make sure that any staff you employ are also aware of the Data Protection Act requirements.

Individuals have rights under the Data Protection Act. They can ask to see the personal data that is held on them, and they have the right to have it corrected if it is wrong. Your company may be sent a 'subject access request', which is a request to show an individual what personal data you hold on them. If you receive a subject access request you are obliged to:

- respond to it within 40 days;
- provide a copy and a description of the data you hold on them;
- advise what the source of the data was;
- give information on how the data is processed;
- give information on which other people or organisations it may have been disclosed to.

The Act requires businesses, which process personal data, to register with ('notify') the Information Commissioner unless they are exempt. Notification is for one year so you will need to renew annually. Failure to notify is a criminal offence. You may be exempt if you only process personal information for core business purposes, such as your own marketing, staff administration or invoicing. The Information Commissioner's website provides an online self-assessment or a downloadable self-assessment guide to help you determine whether notification is required.

The Data Protection Act has a direct connection with information security. One principle states that '*appropriate security measures shall be taken against unauthorised access to, or alteration, disclosure or destruction of personal data, and against accidental loss or destruction of personal data*'. If you are a business user at home and store personal data you need to pay attention to security, and show that your security is in place to meet the requirements of the Act. For further information, check the website of the Information Commissioner at www.ico.gov.uk.

Malicious Communications Act (1988)

This Act makes it an offence to send a message intended to cause distress or anxiety. This might be in the form of a threat, offensive material or abuse of some form.

The Computer Misuse Act (1990)

This Act is intended to deal with hackers. It deals with unauthorised access to, or modification of, computer material. It created the offence of Unauthorised Access. To prove an offence has taken place it must be shown that the access was deliberate, unauthorised and the person committing the act knew it to be unauthorised. A prosecution does not need to show that the access was targeting any particular file or program or even a specific computer. Unauthorised access to anything is sufficient. For this reason it is advisable that any computer system tells users at login that access is intended for the use of authorised persons only. The scope of this Act is quite broad, potentially including any attempt to interfere with the operation of a computer system or the integrity of computer data. A more serious offence was also created that covers unauthorised access with intent to commit a crime. This might cover the use of hacking to steal credit card numbers that are then intended to be used fraudulently.

Regulation of Investigatory Powers Act (2000)

This Act specifies on what grounds, and by whom, traffic on postal and telecommunications networks may be intercepted. It applies to anyone involved in managing network traffic whenever the content of a message becomes known to anyone other than the sender and the receiver. The purposes to which intercepted traffic may be put are also restricted, so if you think it may be necessary to monitor employees' communications you should check that you act within the relevant laws. Monitoring for business purposes, such as to ensure compliance with acceptable use policies, is only permitted if users have been informed, for example. This is covered by the Lawful Business Practice Regulations: www.legislation.hmso.gov.uk/si/si2000/20002699.htm.

SUMMARY

- Be aware of the increased risks being run when work is brought home, and manage them effectively.

- Read your employer's security policy, or if you have employees make sure you have one and they read it.

- Take great care of laptops, smartphones and other portable devices. Consider encrypting the data on them.

- If running a network, then consider a dedicated computer running a firewall to the internet.

- Check whether you are processing personal data and, if you have a business, make sure you register under the Data Protection Act and follow its principles.

- Legal issues with computers are often quite complex and regularly change. There are several laws that you need to be aware of especially if you run, or are employed by, a small business. As a small business you may not be able to afford legal advice, but you can get very useful information published online by government bodies, such as the Information Commissioner's Office.

- Don't breach copyright by using pirated software. Check the licence conditions of any free software you use.

INDEX

117